HO CHI MINH
and His Vietnam

HO CHI MINH
and His Vietnam
A Personal Memoir

Jean Sainteny

Translated from the French by Herma Briffault

Cowles Book Company, Inc.
A subsidiary of Henry Regnery Company
Chicago

Originally published in France as *Face à Ho Chi Minh*.
Copyright © Editions Seghers, Paris, 1970.
English translation copyright © Cowles Book
    Company, Inc., 1972.
Published by Cowles Book Company, Inc., a subsidiary of
Henry Regnery Company, 114 West Illinois Street,
Chicago, Illinois 60610.
Manufactured in the United States of America
Library of Congress Catalog Card Number: 72–183826

Contents

Introduction: The People's Farewell to
their Leader   vii

1   Youthful Ho Voyages West to Europe   1

2   The Vietnamese Nation   5

3   First Combats   11

4   Vietnam during World War II   31

5   First Contacts   41

6   Dialogues with Ho Chi Minh   51

7   In France   69

8   Breakdown of the Peace Negotiations   83

9   Eight Years Later   103

10   Ho Chi Minh and His Followers   123

11   An Attempt at Peaceful Coexistence   135

12   Final Dialogues   161

Appendix 1   Last Will and Testament
of President Ho Chi Minh   167

Appendix 2   Funeral Oration read by Comrade
Le Duan, First Secretary of the
Central Committee of the Workers'
Party of Vietnam, at the Memorial
Service for Ho Chi Minh   171

Appendix 3   Chronology of Important Events
That Affected the Modern History
of Vietnam   177

Index   183

INTRODUCTION:
THE PEOPLE'S FAREWELL
TO THEIR LEADER

Sᴇᴘᴛᴇᴍʙᴇʀ 9, 1969, Hanoi. By eight o'clock in the morning the funeral ceremonies for Ho Chi Minh were over, and the gravely silent crowd that had packed the Ba Dinh public square since early dawn poured out into the avenues, surging back toward the city outskirts and the small suburbs like the ebb-tide that was just then draining the delta of the Red River.

The people had stood quietly in the square or at the crossroads, listening in reverent silence to the funeral oration broadcast over the loud speakers, the farewell address to the leader they had believed immortal. Le Duan, First Secretary of the *Lao Dong*, the Workers' party, had read the speech, drawn up with respect, by his colleagues, in a steady voice only now and then shaken with emotion.*

---

* See Appendix 2 for the complete text of this funeral oration.

vii

Following the oration, the drum and bugle band, whose immaculate white uniforms would have done honor to the most military nation, had played some patriotic hymns (including the "Internationale"). Finally, the "Hymn to the Leader" was sung, and the emotion of the people found release. Until then the crowd had broken the silence only to repeat in chorus the pledges, nearly every one of which was concerned with the reunification of Vietnam, uttered by Le Duan in the name of the departed leader. But now the sound of weeping accompanied and prolonged the closing song, which had been composed in honor of the revered dead leader.

At the first words of "Hymn to the Leader," Premier Pham Van Dong had suddenly broken down and wept, shaken by violent sobs as he stood on the platform, for he had lost, in Ho Chi Minh, not only a fighter-comrade but a teacher and leader, a father figure at whose side or in whose shelter he had for many years borne the burden of state affairs.

A big spectacle, this ceremony was conducted in the purest style of popular governments, but it was of unusual brevity. It had lasted only thirty-five minutes, in compliance with the wishes expressed by Ho Chi Minh. In his last will and testament he had stipulated that neither time nor money should be wasted in an elaborate State funeral.*

Present at these ceremonies were the representatives of the various Communist parties of the world; some thirty delegations had stood there under the hot sun of the late Tonkin summer. I led the delegation from France, the only Western nation represented.

The day before, when it was our turn to file past the glass

---

* See Appendix 1 for complete text of Ho Chi Minh's last will and testament.

coffin where reposed the fragile remains of the old fighter, we had added our offering to the ocean of flowers that covered all the chairs in the great hall of the Ba Dinh palace. The wreath we presented was meant to show the esteem France had for her former adversary and for her determination to forget the past and look calmly toward the future. The admirable simplicity of that ceremony and the grave tone of the funeral march, which set the mood for the procession of the delegates toward the podium, could leave no one unmoved. When it was my turn to pause reverently beside the coffin, I myself could scarcely contain my tears. That emotion stayed with me as the carriage of the Finance Minister of the Democratic Republic of Vietnam bore me back to the French Residence.

And yet I needed no reminder other than the sight of a young sapling, more slender than the other trees in the Avenue Trang Tri down which we drove; that sapling alone would have taken me back twenty-three years to an unforgettable day and would have altered my mood of melancholy—to conjure up the bloodstained past. I saw, in my mind's eye, that avenue plunged into sudden darkness that blacked out the town. Once again I saw myself in the machine gun carrier that was taking me to the fort at which General Morlière was expecting me; once more I felt it shatter under me as a mine we had struck exploded. In flames, riddled with hand grenades, the carrier crashed at the end of the avenue, felling trees, smashing storefronts, and ejecting me and my compansions pell-mell, living torches, onto the sidewalk. Almost at once blood and flames covered the avenue.

That was December 19, 1946. Pho Trang Tri was at that time called the Avenue Borgnis Desbordes, and the explosion was the signal that began a war France was to fight for eight years. The end of that war still cannot be predicted.

Was the man whose funeral I had just attended in 1969 the instigator of that 1946 outrage? Could that attack have been ordered by the man so revered by his people, so esteemed by many others? Or had he merely resigned himself to the inevitable? These questions are unanswered and will probably remain so for some time to come. There are many such questions about the baffling Ho Chi Minh.

I shall not attempt to give all the answers here. Portraying a historical figure is always a challenge, is always something of a gamble, particularly when the subject of the portrait is as inscrutable as Ho Chi Minh, whose life, either willfully or by force of circumstances, was cloaked in mystery. Either by nature or as a matter of tactics he confided in no one. He seems to have had no private life but to have lived solely for the cause to which he was completely dedicated—the independence and reunification of Vietnam.

When the disturbing events of 1945* caused me to be sent to Indochina to negotiate with Ho Chi Minh, I had and sporadically during the next twenty-four years, until his death, continued to have many opportunities to talk with him. I am reputed to be among the very few Occidentals who knew him well, and on many occasions he showed that he trusted me. But all this was not enough to penetrate the mystery of this man, who, even after he had attained power and celebrity status, continued to lead a life of Spartan simplicity.

---

* In 1940 Japan occupied Vietnam and used it as a base for the invasion of Malaysia. A number of Nationalist groups formed the Vietminh (Independence League), headed by Ho Chi Minh, a Communist guerrilla leader. In August, 1945 (at the end of World War II), the Vietminh forced out Bao Dai, the former emperor of Annam and head of a short-lived régime sponsored by Japan. France, seeking to re-establish colonial rule, was to battle the Communist and Nationalist forces from 1946 to May 8, 1954.—*Translator's note.*

After Ho Chi Minh emerged from concealment and attained the eminence he was to maintain for twenty-four years as President of North Vietnam, some of his former comrades in the struggle for independence wrote books about him. But these were designed to edify; they are less biographical than hagiographical in nature, and they unavoidably misrepresent their hero, blur his image, and lay the groundwork for a legend.

Only Ho Chi Minh himself could have recounted his story. Apparently he did not; instead he yielded to the temptation to let his personality remain clouded and impenetrable. Not that he was vain or desired to occupy the center of the stage. Nor did he, like so many Asian and Communist leaders, encourage the "cult of personality." He was a modest man, and if he allowed his biographers to indulge in panegyric, it was not out of a desire to leave a flattering portrait of himself but rather out of a desire to bequeath an example to his people.

My only effort in this book will be to recall the meetings and conversations I had with Ho Chi Minh and thus to give the reader glimpses of him, some impressions that will be more subtle and complex than those presented in official biographies.

At what moment did I confront the real Ho Chi Minh? At what moment did an assumed personality intervene between us? Now, more than twenty-four years since our first encounter, I still find it hard to determine.

In order to be quite honest I shall speak only of the man I really knew, with whom I effectively and interminably conversed. The other aspects, the other phases of his existence, are not entirely unknown to me, but I shall mention them only when to do so will help to depict his character.

What I want to do here is to bear witness. I leave to the historians the task of reconstructing the life of Ho Chi Minh in detail, of examining his acts and judging the effect they must have had in Asia and elsewhere. Some historians have already set themselves to that task; many others will undertake it in the future. If these pages can help them to accomplish their aim, I shall have accomplished mine.

HO CHI MINH
and His Vietnam

1

YOUTHFUL HO VOYAGES WEST TO EUROPE

1911. The merchant marine vessel the *Latouche-Tréville* cast off her moorings and slowly headed out into the Saigon River.

A few minutes earlier, the relatives, friends, and creditors* of the passengers leaving for France had descended the gangplanks and were loitering on the docks in the sweltering hot night of Cochin China, trying to keep in sight as long as possible the faces of those they had accompanied on board and who, it seemed to those who remained, were already in France, despite the four long weeks it would take the ship to reach the motherland.

---

* At that time everyone seemed to live on credit in Indochina, as elsewhere in the Far East, and the tradespeople never missed the departure of a boat, hoping to catch a debtor who had neglected to pay a part or all of his debts.

The members of the crew not on duty mingled with the passengers on deck. Passengers and crew alike were mainly Annamites, and they too waved goodbye to the people who had come to wish them a *bon voyage*.

Among the crew members was a slender young man standing alone, silent and self-contained. He gazed fixedly at these docks in this French city of Indochina and, beyond the plateau it climbs, at the back-country, which, though hidden in the darkness, he knew to be there under the starry sky.

That young man, in 1911, was still called Nguyen Tat Thanh. Later he would also bear the names Ly Thui, Linov, Tong Van So, and Nguyen Ai Quoc. History would eventually know him as Ho Chi Minh.

Having very soon realized that it was hopeless to struggle for the emancipation of his country from France, surrounded by those whose precise mission or interest was to oppose such a thing—government functionaries and French colonials—Nguyen Tat Thanh had decided to travel in France and elsewhere in Europe. His intention was to become better acquainted with the adversary he would eventually have to confront. He also intended to seek help from certain Frenchmen and, if possible, from certain powers, whether friendly or hostile to France, whether suspicious or envious of her colonial possessions.

"Don't waste your breath explaining to me that we were better off under French rule," this mandarin's son was to tell me thirty-five years later. "Perhaps we were. But we still prefer, as you say in France, to tighten our belts and be free. You should understand this, for you were among those who struggled against the occupation of your country by the Nazis."

Thus early in life this scholar and son of a scholar chose privation to subjection. From his very first voyage to the

Western world as a mere boy, he was resolved to earn his living by no matter what humble employment. When he first decided to go to France in order to find a way to achieve his country's independence, he had urged a childhood friend to accompany him. "But where will you get the money for this?" the friend had asked. Ho Chi Minh answered, spreading out his delicate scholar's hands, "The money is there."

The anecdote may be, like so many others about Ho Chi Minh, postfabricated, but it nonetheless depicts his character. On the voyage from Saigon to Le Havre, he worked his way as a mess-boy, dubbed by the rest of the crew "the student," in the galleys of the *Latouche-Tréville.*

His work as a mess-boy was the first of a series of humble and often disheartening jobs he held to enable him to survive and to act politically when the right moment arrived.

And this way of life, pursued for a half century in Europe and Asia, was endured by him always and everywhere with but one goal: the independence of Vietnam.

But what is Vietnam?

2

THE VIETNAMESE
NATION

Vietnam is a nation profoundly rooted in a history of more than twenty centuries,* proud of its past, its traditions, and its individuality and capable of doing anything necessary to preserve them.

When people are astounded at the extraordinary resistance put up by this small country, first against France and now against the powerful United States, it is perhaps because they do not know that Vietnam held out in the thirteenth century against the invincible Kublai Khan, thus limiting the Mongol expansion in Asia.

---

* In the eulogy he read at Ho Chi Minh's funeral, Le Duan, First Secretary of the party, spoke not of two thousand years but of "four thousand years," thus espousing the theory of certain students of Vietnam history, based on recent archaeological finds. See Appendix 2.

Geography has played a prime role. Virtually no other nation has felt as much as Vietnam the influence of and, likewise, the consequences of its geographical situation.

Widely exposed to the Pacific Ocean—two great rivers emptying there—Vietnam is a demarcation line between two ancient civilizations (Chinese and Indian), which profoundly shaped its ethnic, historical, cultural, and political destiny.

The Vietnamese people, born in prehistoric times as a result of the fusions of Mongols, Melanesians, and Indonesians, became an ethnic entity at about the beginning of the third century B.C.

Lying to the north of the peninsula, the nation was at first confined to that delta of the Red River that we call Tonkin. But the Vietnamese people were not long in extending their domain and empire toward the south, all along the narrow coastal plain wedged between the China Sea and the Annamese mountain chain; for Tonkin has never been capable of feeding its population.

Placed at the center of the coast bordering the southern China Sea—the Asiatic Mediterranean—Vietnam has Indonesia to the south, Malaysia to the west, the Philippines to the east. To the north Vietnam is dominated in every sense of the word by a common frontier with China. That overpowering proximity weighs more heavily on its destiny than anything else.

Thus, if Vietnam, because of its territorial expansion, gained a certain power and influence, it was at the same time rendered vulnerable by that very increase of territory, the length of its shoreline, and the openness of its frontiers. As Philippe Devillers has written, Vietnam was destined "to live dangerously."

In fact, the geographical characteristics of Vietnam have obliged this little nation to struggle almost continually to preserve its territorial integrity. It has been a struggle on two fronts, exterior and interior, one to oppose the aggressions and invasions of neighboring countries, the other to control military operations designed to assimilate or annihilate the tribes, the villages, or the principalities that contested the extension of its authority.

In the fifteenth century, for example, Vietnam succeeded in absorbing the kingdom of Champa to the south. However, weakened by this costly victory, Vietnam fell under the tutelage of China, a "protection" from which it had escaped in the tenth century after suffering it for nine hundred years. Time and again Vietnam would succeed in shaking off that yoke but only for brief periods and never completely.* Indeed, in 1884 and 1885 France had to force China to recognize the French protectorate over Annam and Tonkin.

Practically indifferent to the French conquest of Cochin China, the southern tip of the Indochinese peninsula, and indifferent to a certain extent even to the French protectorate in Annam, the Chinese government had reacted vigorously to French enterprises in the region of Tonkin. A Chinese document of 1882 describes Tonkin thus: "Barrier of the Middle Empire, small nation which serves to protect the provinces of Yunnan and Kuang-si. . . . Although situated outside the Empire, we cannot abandon it. . . ."**

---

* Historians count four periods of avowed Chinese domination of Vietnam: from 1110 B.C. to 43 A.D.; from 44 A.D. to 543; from 603 to 938; and from 1407 to 1427.

** Aware of this, the French Minister of the Marine advised the Governor-General of Vietnam not to permit himself to be drawn into a conflict at Tonkin.

The Chinese anxieties were justified. From the moment that Tonkin passed under French control a new epoch began in the history of Vietnam. It was only during the French colonial period that Vietnam was really able to elude the grasp of her redoubtable neighbor.

Ironically, then, during this period of "French peace," Vietnam took advantage of it to prepare for the struggle against France!

It is an old story, to be found in all parts of the world, but it seems to apply particularly to Vietnam, where every contemporary event seems to repeat one or many other such events in the past.

When, for example, in 949 Vietnam had succeeded in liberating herself from ten centuries of Chinese domination, it was because China was a divided, weakened empire, susceptible to anarchy following the crumbling of the Tang dynasty. And when, in 1944, the Vietnamese undertook to liberate themselves from French tutelage, it was because they knew France was weakened and bruised at the end of World War II and unable to attend to all of her overseas possessions as a result of the material and moral damages inflicted by that war.

Again, when, in 1884, the France of Jules Ferry was shaken by the Langson affair, it was because Chinese troops from the Baclay post pretended not to have received notice of the accord France had signed in Tientsin with their government. Consequently, when they opened fire on the French column that was moving toward Langson as a result of the Franco-Chinese accord, they took the column by surprise.

A recent example of this sort of event comes to mind. When, on March 6, 1946, the French fleet that was bearing General Leclerc and his armored car division to Tonkin, was subjected to Chinese fire at Haiphong, it was because the Chinese had not been informed of the accord signed by the French with their government at Thung-king on February 28.

The Chinese then, as formerly, tried to oppose by every means the French conquest, or reconquest (even peaceful), of Tonkin, which protected their southern provinces and which they had never completely renounced. (It should not be forgotten that the Chinese had obtained from the Americans the promise that after World War II North Vietnam would once more find its place in the Chinese "zone of influence.")

A matter for speculation at the present writing is whether or not North Vietnam, in exhausting herself in the war against the United States—as she exhausted herself earlier in the conquest of Champa—does not risk becoming an all-too-easy prey of her hereditary suzerain.

The bloody and fratricidal war between North Vietnam and South Vietnam that we are witnessing today also has its counterpart in Vietnamese history. Beyond the immediate causes that provoked or furthered the conflict (the division of the country by the Geneva Accords, ideological differences, foreign interventions) deeper causes have for a long time tended to split the two Vietnams, with the expansionist North sending conquerors down to the southern states (Champa, Cochin China, even Cambodia) with the aim of absorbing them totally or in part.

That conquest achieved, this traditional opposition continues in the rivalry of the Trinh, lords of the North, and the Nguyen, lords of the South. In this fratricidal struggle each contestant labels the other "foreign."

Many years ago this desperate struggle impelled the Nguyen, who were threatened by five thousand men and five hundred elephants of the Trinh army, to appeal to the Western powers for help—first Portugal, then France. It required all the authority and cleverness of Nguyen Anh, who was to become the great emperor Gia Long (powerfully aided by French missionary Pigneau de Béhaine, Bishop of Adran), to put an end to the rivalries of those furious Nationalists. Today we see that this pacification was only a brief interlude.

The Vietnamese are rightfully proud of their significant martial history. But such national pride is dangerous and generates conflicts when it is not tempered by the wisdom of national leaders.

Fortunately that wisdom is also a fruit of the territory and is not lacking in the men produced in Vietnam. Conquerors by necessity as much as by temperament, the Vietnamese have shown throughout their history that they know how to abandon the sword for the plowshare, how to turn their soldiers into growers of rice, and how to govern their conquered lands with a sense of organization that was so admired by the first Western travelers in the Orient. It is these precedents that offer hope for their future.

3

FIRST COMBATS

Just as it is indispensable for an understanding of the Vietnamese character to know the history and geography of the country, it is necessary also to consider the provincial and family background that formed Ho Chi Minh if one is to have any hope of understanding his personality.

Besides, it is perhaps in the Nghe-an region, where Ho Chi Minh was born, that the qualities that make up the Vietnamese people are most marked.

This disinherited region, with poor soil and a climate of extremes, demands, like nearly all of North Annam, an exceptional endurance of its sons. "Green waters, blue mountains," the songs describe it. There are also many forests, but there are few arable plains. In summer a torrid wind dries the earth and burns the vegetation. In autumn there are diluvial rains and typhoons so violent that at times the rivers change their course. Thus, Nghe-an has nurtured a hard-working, dependable, and frugal people, at times brimming with poetic imagination. It is a race less frank and charming than the peoples of Annam and Cochin China, but it is one that compels admiration for its obstinacy, inventiveness, faculties of assimilation, and fidelity to national traditions. It is a race forged through two thousand years of conquest, of the defense and development of a land that is pitiless to the weak and to those who have not been born there.

These qualities of the North Vietnamese were the most significant qualities of Ho Chi Minh. He proved it throughout his life, right up to his death, by exhibiting an energy and a range of activity incredible in a man whose frail appearance periodically gave rise to rumors of his decease from exhaustion or sickness—rumors easily believed because they appeared so likely.

The child named Cung was born in 1890 in the village of Chua, in the subprefecture of Nam-dan. The youngest of a family of three children—two boys, one girl—that child, who was to become known as Ho Chi Minh, President of the Democratic Republic of Vietnam, lost his mother at the age of ten. He was brought up by his father, Nguyen Dinh Sac, an unusual man and a self-educated scholar. As a boy he had herded water buffalo, but he eventually became a mandarin after passing the triennial examination and obtaining the degree of Doctor of Chinese Letters, second grade.

After teaching for a time, Ho's father became a government functionary, first in Hué, the capital at that time of the Annam empire, and later in the district of Binh-dinh, where he was subprefect. Dismissed from office on spurious charges in about 1915, Nguyen Dinh Sac kept himself and his family alive by whatever means he could, wandering from place to place, teaching Chinese and giving consultations in native medicine. He was to be seen for a long time in Saigon, in the Rue Lagrandière, where he wrote out his medical prescriptions in the shelter of a Chinese booth. He was also seen in the ruins of Anghor, to which he had traveled on foot, a distance of about four hundred miles. Long before his son was called "Uncle," this title of respect was bestowed upon Nguyen Dinh Sac.

According to some reports, Nguyen Dinh Sac had been dismissed from the French administration for intemperance and peculation; according to others, he was dismissed because of his anti-French attitude. Certainly the father of the future Ho Chi Minh refused to speak French (he did not learn French until he was fifty) and had suspicious relations with the colonial police. Worse, he was in contact with the revolutionary Phan Chau Trinh, who had escaped the death penalty only because of the intervention of the League of the Rights of Man, and with old Phan Boi Chau, another adversary of French colonialism, who enjoyed great prestige in the Opposition sectors of the public.

Certainly Nguyen Dinh Sac's dismissal and his activities profoundly influenced the destiny of the little boy Cung. Moreover, we know that, like his brother and sister, Cung was subjected to the influence of another Nationalistic relative, his great-uncle, who was for many years the comrade of the famous Hoa Than (called De Tham) and himself a redoubtable opponent of the French administration, having led guerilla attacks on French troops before he was assassinated in 1913.

We must not forget the years passed in Hué, when the child Cung lived with his family in a dark one-room apartment facing the Palais de la Censure, which must have made him keenly aware of the contrast between the poverty of the native people and the luxurious wealth of the imperial court. He also had to endure the mockery of his better-dressed comrades, well-fed sons of traditional mandarins who laughed at him, with his peasant tunic and his Nghe-an way of wearing his hair in two knots on top of his head.

"Nothing is more contemptible than to seek honors through literature." These lines by the poet Tuy Vien were to be adopted as a maxim by young Cung, and he often repeated the words to Phan Boi Chau, who had originally repeated them to him.

Cung was not a grind at school; he would not be one of those "collaborating" mandarins loaded with honors that merely represented, said his father, "the *nec plus ultra* of slavery." But all the same he would be, in accordance with the tradition of his native land, an intellectual and a Nationalist. The province of Nghe-an, which had earned the title of "rebel province," never ceased to supply members of the élite to the Vietnamese nation: scholars, poets, reformers, and inspirers of patriotic uprisings.

It was also in North Annam that the first important rebellion against the French broke out, in 1885, in the first year of the French protectorate. An uprising of the mandarins, in history it is known as "the revolt of the scholars."

If one was to make a list of all the men native to that province who ever rebelled against the French presence, it would be a long one—as long perhaps as that listing all the revolts that took place during the twenty preceding centuries against the Chinese. But if history retains only one of those names, it may be safely predicted that the name chosen will be that of Ho Chi Minh, the child Cung, born in May, 1890, in the village of Chua.

One of Ho Chi Minh's biographers has portrayed him by calling upon compatriot witnesses, people who knew him in the various foreign countries where he lived, to report the events of his life. These narratives sound like an amalgam of the catechism and moral tales for the young, and they show the future President of the Democratic Republic of Vietnam continually preaching to his interlocutors, by parable or aphorism, saying such things as "Better to keep your money for spending on travel and instruction than to spend it at the seaside with the girls. . . ."

Tran Ngoc Danh, throughout his *Histoire du Président Ho,* published in 1949, strains similarly to confirm the virtuous and ascetic but meek and mild aspects of the man who was to become known as "the good Uncle Ho."

One of these exemplary tales shows him in Thailand, where he had been drawn by the presence of some twenty thousand of his compatriots* whom he wanted to catechize. Ho Chi Minh chose to lead the life of a lay monk. In fact, it may not have been merely to avoid being captured that Ho Chi Minh was pleased to wear the saffron robes of Buddhist priests when going from one friendly society or union to another, encouraging his Vietnamese compatriots to instruct and cultivate themselves—in short, to arm themselves intellectually. In any case, he did set an example by employing his time rigorously, with impeccable discipline and faultless punctuality (habits he always preserved). Manual work of the most strenuous kind alternated with the study of the local language and with conferences on political formation. Too, Ho Chi Minh organized theatricals (very like the ancient "Mysteries"), in which he always played a part.

At this period of his life he composed a hymn, and when he traveled throughout the country, followed by a few disciples, he recited the *Kieu*** or some Vietnamese folk poem,

---

* The number approaches one hundred thousand today.

** The *Kieu* is a classic of Vietnamese literature, and the author is a native of the Nghe-an province.

which his followers recited after him. They used this device to overcome fatigue and to strengthen their souls. In order to keep up their bodily strength these pilgrims had to be satisfied with the leftovers of food at the temples of the bonzes, whose meals were more than frugal.

We have seen how, while working his way as mess-boy on the *Latouche-Tréville*, the youthful Cung acquired his title "the student." But he also was given another name, "Ba," the name he had given the purser upon embarking. His impressions on this first voyage to the west were varied. He was shocked at the boldness of some pretty female passengers, was touched by the kindness of two young Frenchmen who were returning to France, and at Marseilles was astounded to see poor women on the quays gathering up the grains of rice or maize that had spilled out of torn sacks. He was agreeably surprised when a tavern keeper addressed him as "Monsieur," but he was troubled to see his co-workers joking familiarly with the waitress and playing card games incessantly.

At Sainte-Adresse, Ba found work in various kitchens. He had some good employers and a satisfactory job that left him some leisure time, which he spent reading everything he could find, studying to perfect his French, and working in a flower garden. His biographers picture him at this time as a very thin young man, badly dressed but extremely polite.

More voyages followed that first one. He embarked as chief cook on a cargo boat that skirted the African coasts. At the French ports of call Ba encountered once again "bad Frenchmen," who scandalously exploited the poor natives. His assistant cook has recorded some of his remarks. "In France," Ho said, "the French are very good; but in the colonies these Frenchmen are very mean, very inhuman. . . . For these colonials, the life of yellow or black people doesn't count at all."

On this cargo boat Ba had difficulties with the crew, for he objected to their stealing wine from the hold and getting drunk. He showed his disapproval by refusing to take part in their carousals, or so his adulating chroniclers report. They recount also how during this voyage he always rose before daybreak to enjoy the sunrises and never went to bed when moonlight illumined the ocean.

In short, his life is reported to have been an exemplary one that all Vietnamese people should know, admire, and imitate.

Ba voyaged to Boston and New York, where he spent some time, but little is known of his American experiences. He traveled to London, and there, after working as a day laborer, shoveling snow, tending boilers, and so on, he eventually found enjoyable employment in the kitchens of the fashionable Hotel Carlton, where the prestigious Escoffier was the chef.

While learning English, as one of his compatriots has recorded, Ba was treated well by the pastry chef, who taught him the art of pastry making. So expert did Ba become in this skill that Escoffier was extremely concerned to learn that the new apprentice intended to sacrifice a promising career in cuisine by going into politics.

When World War I broke out, Ba tried to enlist in the British army, but he was rejected as physically unfit. Unable to serve, he put all his savings into national defense bonds.

Then he returned to France.

Unfortunately it is from these and other naive panegyrics that have come down to us that we must draw the material for portraying Ho Chi Minh's youthful years. He was both less good and much better than this coloring-book picture of him would have us believe.

Perhaps later Ho Chi Minh would realize that the simplicity of his life and the strictness of his morals contributed to his popularity with the masses, but in these early years his abstemiousness and self-discipline were practiced out of sheer necessity. He simply adapted himself to the privations imposed upon him by the existence he had freely chosen.

More detailed information exists in regard to Ba's stay in Paris—where he assumed the name Nguyen Ai Quoc ("He who loves his country"), the name by which he was known for many years. In Paris, as usual, he took any employment that was available, and for some time he was a retoucher of photographs. After that he worked as an artist designing "Asian antiquities" made in France.

The lodgings he shared with compatriots were always poverty-stricken, situated in the poorest neighborhoods of the capital. One of his addresses was in the Rue Compaint, a street in the Batignolles district.

Physical privations did not matter; what he wanted was to educate himself. He frequented workers' clubs; he joined artistic and scientific societies, tourist associations, anything that would permit him to visit factories, museums and theaters and to take instructive trips. He traveled occasionally to Italy and to Switzerland, which, by contrast, impressed him with its democracy, tolerance, and hygiene.

But above all, he read. He read with application and enthusiasm, he read assiduously in the libraries, and he set aside the major part of his earnings for the purchase of books, especially those concerning political science. It was at this time that he ran across a book that overwhelmed him: Karl Marx's *Das Kapital*. Soon it was his bedside book, his nightly companion.

The adherence of the young Nguyen Ai Quoc to communism was unrestricted, complete. We can say this with certitude.

Some commentaries on Ho Chi Minh's life place this event earlier, while he was still in Vietnam. For my part I align myself with those who think he made this fundamental choice when his mind had matured and when he was seeking a way to achieve the goal that had become his *raison d'être:* the independence of Vietnam from colonial rule.

In addition, he himself declared this in an article that has become famous, published in 1960 by the periodical *L'Echo du Vietnam* on the occasion of his seventieth birthday. The reference to the Parisian newspaper *l'Humanité* surely places his conversion to communism in the period of his youth when he was in Paris.

> A comrade gave me some essays of Lenin to read; they concerned the problem of nationalities and colonial peoples and were published by *l'Humanité*. Some political terms in them puzzled me. But by reading and rereading the pamphlets many times, I finally grasped the essential. And I was filled with a great enthusiasm and a great faith that helped me to see the problems clearly. I was so happy over this that I sometimes wept. Alone in my room I exclaimed aloud, as if addressing a mass meeting: "Dear oppressed and unhappy compatriots!" I cried, "Here is the road to your liberation!"

It was a revelation.

Perhaps we should take note that a young assistant librarian in Peking also found "the road" at about this same time. He was twenty-four years old, and his name was Mao Tse-tung. An idealistic reformer as well as a patriot, Mao suffered as the future Ho Chi Minh suffered over the affronts inflicted on his native land by the Western powers. The head librarian at the University of Peking, a certain Li-Ta-Chao, introduced Mao to the writings of Marx and Lenin and to works on the Russian Revolution. Mao became convinced that Chinese capitalism, allied with foreign interests, was largely responsible for the decadence and servitude of his country. No doubt it was the essential reason for his xeno-phobia, and this extreme of patriotism has now captured the entire Chinese population.*

The two great leaders were destined not to meet until much later, after their double conversion had already taken place. Ho Chi Minh, like Mao, became a Communist in 1917. But clearly for him communism was at first largely a means of attaining the goal of the independence of his country.

I have been asked countless times, "Was Ho Chi Minh pri-marily a Nationalist or a Communist?" My reply is always the same: Ho Chi Minh was both. For him nationalism and communism were, respectively, goal and the means to attain that goal. The two complemented each other, merged.

Nguyen Ai Quoc initiated his political career in 1918 at the conference of the Treaty of Versailles. With two compatriots he undertook to address a demand to Clemenceau, Lloyd George, and Wilson: "Notes on the revindications of the Annamese people." It was a kind of eight-point plan that de-nounced the colonial exploitation of the Vietnamese people and recommended a certain measure of independence for Vietnam. He tried to obtain an audience with Wilson but with no more success than the author had. The hour was not yet ripe for Americans to decolonize the possessions of their allies, and Versailles was neither Yalta nor Potsdam.

Nguyen Ai Quoc returned to journalism. Charles Longuet, of the *Populaire*, encouraged him to write articles that would reveal to the French people the injustices committed by their

---

* Possibly Lenin's promise to "abolish the unequal treaties" by which Czarist Russia had acquired the territories to the east of the Ussuri River also played a part in young Mao's espousal of Leninism. If so, it is ironic, as recent events have reminded us, that those terri-tories, more than sixty years after the Russian Revolution, are still in Russia's possession.

representatives in Indochina. Even though he had been nurtured on Hugo, Zola, and Michelet, the style most appreciated by Nguyen Ai Quoc was devoid of ornament:

To see something, to feel something, then to write about it; to try to discern the appearance and reality of things, then express them. That is all there is to it, surely? Then what is do difficult about writing?

However, he still experienced some difficulty in writing in the French language, and at first, not a little impatiently, he had to resign himself to dictating his articles to compatriots better acquainted with the intricacies and subtleties of French.

Nguyen Ai Quoc, as the first Vietnamese inscribed in the books of the French Socialist party, was soon noticed by Marcel Cachin, who invited him in 1920 to attend the Congress at Tours, where the Socialists, as it happened, separated from the Second International and joined the Third International.

From then on, for many years all the activities of Nguyen Ai Quoc would be cast in this mold. One would have thought that his temperament should have held him to the Socialist ranks, which were opposed to violence, but he had been very disappointed by the Socialist attitude at the Congress at Tours. In his opinion the Socialists wasted their time in sterile and theoretical discussions instead of spending it profitably by agitating for the only cause that interested him—the independence of the French colonies, particularly Indochina.

He had also been exasperated by (one of his compatriots has said "disgusted with") the cautious "wait and see" attitude of some old Vietnamese revolutionaries (Phan Chau Trinh and Phan Van Truong, among others) whom he had encountered in Paris and who dismissed as "childishness" his and his comrades' enthusiasm.

In contrast, Moscow seemed ready for action. From its very creation the Third International had proclaimed the necessity of parallel action in the capitals and their "dependencies." In July, 1920, Moscow had convened a congress of Oriental peoples at Baku in the Crimea. In Moscow the Lenin Institute was training revolutionary cadres. In Shanghai an office of the Far East was created. And so on.

What part did Nguyen Ai Quoc play in the Third International? Jean Lacouture, in his remarkable biography of Ho Chi Minh, has drawn upon all existing sources, so we may consult his findings.

Between the years 1920 and 1923, while still in Paris, Nguyen Ai Quoc created what was called The Intercolonial Union, destined to gather together all the anticolonial organizations in the French Empire. He founded and managed a periodical with the significant name of *Le Paria* (*The Outcast*), in which he published articles brimful of passion and occasional ruthlessness that testify not only to his intelligence and humor but to the perfect knowledge of the French language he had acquired (as he had and was publishing in the Communist daily newspaper *l'Humanité*).

In 1923 he was in Moscow first under the name Ly Thuy, then under the name of Linov, as representative of the French colonies on the permanent Committee of the Krestintern (Peasant International). At the University of Oriental Peoples he learned the Russian language and revolutionary strategy. There he encountered some Soviet leaders who were to be useful to him in the future.

In 1925 Ho Chi Minh was sent to Canton as an assistant to Mikhail Borodin, the Comintern envoy to the Chinese revolutionary government, headed at the time by Chiang Kaishek, successor to the great Sun Yat Sen. And in Canton he was placed in charge of the Press Bureau of the Soviet Consulate, but his true mission was to prepare the Communist propaganda and action in Indochina.

The revolutionary tactic of the Third International, as applied by Borodin in China, consisted of the following: primarily to assure the independence of the country and to install, by a Nationalist revolution, a democratic régime; and to integrate that government with the International by means of a second revolution, which would be Communist in nature.

At first, Nguyen Ai Quoc began to apply these concepts to his strategies for his native land. But he soon was made to realize how risky was an alliance with the bourgeois Nationalists—the Kuomintang in China. Until 1927 General Chiang Kai-shek had cooperated with the Communists, but on April 6 of that year he initiated his offensive against them. And the long civil war began.

Because of the war Nguyen Ai Quoc had to flee Canton with Borodin, retreating to the Kuang-Si and from there returning to Moscow. However, his time in Canton had not been wasted. He had met there and converted to his cause a young professor who was to become his most important assistant: Pham Van Dong. There, too, he organized, along with the Kindu Koy and some Koreans, a League of Oppressed Peoples and formed, among the Vietnamese émigrés, a veritable nursery of young Communists called *Thanh Nien* (Youth Corps).

The result of his actions was that beginning in 1926, Nguyen Ai Quoc succeeded in injecting certain of these disciples and philosophical tenets into Indochina and in setting in motion throughout the country a clandestine network that facilitated the circulation of revolutionary agents and their propaganda. These actions provided a necessary infrastructure, for almost everything had to be done to enlighten the Indochinese masses.

In the following year, while in Moscow, Nguyen Ai Quoc was given the task of organizing an Indochinese Communist party, which he said was needed since no one in Indochina at that time even understood the term communism.*

In the 1920s Nguyen Ai Quoc stayed for a short period in Berlin in order to study the rudiments of the German language. A comparison he made between the German and French capitals has been recorded. Berlin, he said, was "like a slice of bread as compared to a slice of cake."

In the early weeks of 1928 Nguyen Ai Quoc returned to the Far East but not to Indochina, for his clandestine activities had come to the notice of the French *Sûreté,* making it dangerous for him to go to Indochina. He settled in Thailand, where he contined his underground work in absolute secrecy. Soon he was put in charge of the propaganda and activities of Communists in Southeast Asia—British and Dutch Malaysia, Thailand, Burma, and, of course, Indochina.

In January, 1930, he was summoned to Hong Kong, and it was there that his consummate political skill was first revealed.

Beginning in May, 1929, the first congress of Indochinese revolutionaries assembled in Hong Kong. The three groups represented were unable to agree on the main points of their program. Moscow wanted, or rather demanded, a fusion of the groups. Hearing of the presence of Nguyen Ai Quoc in Thailand, the dissident groups appealed to him. He arrived

---

* Thirty years later the masses still needed this education. During my second mission to Hanoi, in 1955, my wife's chambermaid at the delegation headquarters had to spend certain hours attending political courses. "De-Stalinization" was then raging, and one day the woman asked my wife, "Madame, who is this Stalin?"

in Hong Kong in January, 1930, called together two delegates of each group, studied the men and the situation, elaborated a program, and drew up the statutes. On February 3, in the course of a single meeting that lasted only a few hours, he settled the dispute and brought about unity.

Thus was created the Vietnam Cong-San Dang, or Indochinese Communist party. Its direction was, quite naturally, offered to Nguyen Ai Quoc.

But Nguyen Ai Quoc accomplished still more during these important years. During the eighteen months that followed, from 1930 to 1931, he traveled indefatigably—from Hong Kong to Shanghai or Bangkok or Hankow—and became known as the virtual head of all the Communist organizations of the Indian archipelago. He assured the liaison of these organizations with the Third International—that is, with Moscow—and with the French Communist party, through the intermediary of the general confederation of workers in Paris—the famous C.G.T. (*Conféderation Générale du Travail*). The archives of that confederation must surely contain some very interesting documents.

Like Mao Tse-tung, Nguyen Ai Quoc realized that Marx's *Das Kapital* could not be followed literally in Asia, where industrial workers are in the minority.* In Asia the peasants would have to be mobilized. Already in 1924, at the Fifth Congress of the International in Moscow, Nguyen Ai Quoc had pointed this out:

> In all the French colonies . . . conditions have combined to further an uprising of the peasants. Here and there they have rebelled, but their rebellions have been drowned in blood.   If the peasants remain pacific today it is because they lack organization and a leader . . . .

---

* In 1928 their number in Indochina was only about fifty thousand.

Neither organization nor leadership would be lacking from then on. And the appearance of a Soviet organization in Nghe-an, the native province of Nguyen Ai Quoc, no doubt explains in great part the peasant uprisings during the summer of 1930.* Because of its poverty the province was ripe for revolution.

The most important manifestation of unrest was the "hunger march" of September 12, 1930, toward the town of Vinh, which brought together approximately six thousand peasants.

The march was a success, but its amplitude was fatal to its organizers, because a harsh repression followed. Hundreds of militants were arrested, and most of them were condemned to death or imprisonment. Pham Van Dong, the present Prime Minister of the Democratic Republic of Vietnam, was among those who were imprisoned in Poulo-Condore.

And as for Nguyen Ai Quoc, in 1931 he was condemned to death *in absentia.*

We have few facts about Ho's life for the succeeding three or four years. Uncertainty surrounds the whereabouts and actions of the rebel condemned to death, and the rumors are conflicting.

According to one rumor, he was arrested on June 6, 1931, by the British police in Hong Kong. (The British, too, had some accounts to settle with him since he was suspected of having fomented disturbances in the Crown colonies.) The French authorities in Indochina then proceeded to negotiate with the British to obtain Nguyen Ai Quoc's extradition. In

---

* This was when I discovered for the first time the discontent existing in the French protectorate. Most French residents in Indochina, especially in Saigon, where I lived in 1930, existed in tranquil ignorance of conditions, convinced that the Annamese were as happy as they in that lovely country.

about 1933 they were told that the person concerned had died of tuberculosis in prison. This death was registered by the *Sûreté* in Hanoi and announced in the Paris newspaper *l'Humanité* and in the Soviet press. In Moscow some Vietnamese students organized a memorial service for the supposedly deceased revolutionary.

In fact, Nguyen Ai Quoc had contracted tuberculosis, but he had not died from it. He had even gathered enough strength to give his British jailers the slip and to outwit the surveillance of the French agents waiting in Hong Kong to capture him upon his release from prison.

How had he escaped and by what means?

It was related in later years that anticolonialist British lawyer Frank Loseby aroused his compatriots in the Labour party, notably Stafford Cripps, the future Chancellor of the Exchequer, in favor of the prisoner and obtained the prisoner's pardon from the Crown Council in London. Then apparently Frank Loseby somehow aided Nguyen Ai Quoc to flee secretly from Hong Kong.

But still another theory has been advanced.

According to a second version, Nguyen Ai Quoc obtained his pardon in payment for some services he had rendered the British Intelligence Service. But this theory seems incompatible with what we know of Nguyen Ai Quoc's character.

The only certainty in all this mystery is that the hero of the episode later paid homage to the British for their generous treatment of him. Frenchmen will continue to ponder that strange attitude of the British authorities in that instance.

At any rate, in 1933 it was less possible than ever for Nguyen Ai Quoc to return to Indochina. He would work tirelessly abroad for the reconstitution of his dismantled political party. For a time he hid out in Shanghai from Chiang Kaishek, who was resuming his persecution of Communists. He was rescued from this impasse by a distinguished Frenchman, Paul Vaillant-Couturier, whom he had met in Paris in the 1920s. Vaillant-Couturier was a member of the central committee of the Communist party, and he managed to secure passage for Nguyen Ai Quoc aboard a Soviet packet headed for Vladivostok.

It seems that Nguyen Ai Quoc remained in Russia from 1934 to 1938, studying at the Lenin Institute and teaching the history of Vietnam. He composed his courses in the form of poems in order to make them more attractive and memorable (this was in imitation of Phan Boi Chau, his teacher, who had formerly issued his revolutionary proclamations in rhyme in order to help the people learn them by heart).

In any case, the First Congress of the Indochinese Communist party was held in 1935 without the presence of Nguyen Ai Quoc. The congress was belligerent, and, in view of the 1930 success, it seemed that armed revolt was likely.

This was not exactly what, three months later, the Seventh Congress of the International would predict; nor was it exactly what at that time Nguyen Ai Quoc advocated. He was too much a realist not to adapt his actions and directives to contingencies. For example, between 1936 and 1938, the period in France of the Popular Front, he ordered his agents to collaborate with and declare loyalty to the French. As will be seen, this was a feature of the methods dear to Ho Chi Minh: always to seize the opportunity of the moment.

In 1938 Nguyen Ai Quoc returned to China. Fear of the Japanese had obliged Chiang Kai-shek to ally himself once more with the Communists in order to fight the invader. Thus the future leader of the Vietminh was for a time given the task of training the soldiers of the Kuomintang in certain aspects of guerrilla warfare.

In the years preceding World War II, Ho's skill as a revolutionary leader was proved. While organizing a legal party grouping of more than five hundred labor unions, committees, corporations, and so on, he cleverly managed to pre-serve the undercover apparatus he had created in Indochina. This success enabled the revolutionaries to subsist and to preserve their influence beyond 1939, when, at the declaration of war, the French authorities in Indochina suppressed the legal party. It also permitted a clandestine action against the Japanese invaders to be carried out in 1940, much to the later political benefit of the Indochinese Communists.

In February, 1940, Nguyen Ai Quoc was able to rejoin a group of the Indochinese Communists in southern China who had been forced to flee when the French suppressed the legal party. Among them were two men who, from then on, never ceased to be his most intimate collaborators: Pham Van Dong, the present Prime Minister of North Vietnam, and Vo Nguyen Giap, future Minister of War, Commander-in-Chief, and victor at Dienbienphu in 1954. They were two strong men if ever there were.

4

VIETNAM DURING
WORLD WAR II

June, 1940. The defeat of France in Europe created a new situation in Asia. The Japanese, Germany's allies, appeared on the Indochinese scene, trying by means of military efforts to control the Chinese-Tonkin frontier. Their intention was to cut off military supplies being sent to their enemies, the Chinese, since these supplies had to cross French territories. In fact, the Japanese wanted to assure also a base of operations in Indochina against the powerful British Crown colony of Singapore and more generally against the southern seas.

Confronted with the deficiencies of the Vichy government and the refusal of aid from Great Britain and the United States (not yet in the war) to furnish arms to oppose the demands of Japan, General Catroux, Governor-General of the French Protectorate, threw in his lot with the Free French.

Admiral Decoux succeeded General Catroux as Governor-General and was soon obliged to let the Japanese move into Indochina.

When we recall the atrocities the Japanese committed later, it must be admitted that they showed some restraint at first. But from 1940, their expansionism was something to fear. Initially they did not hand over Indochina to a vanquished France. Although they were pledged to respect France's sovereignty, they very soon took action against colonial France. Faithful to their politics of emancipation of all Asiatic colonies, they favored the agitation supported by the Nationalists in Vietnam but not, of course, the activities of the Communist party.

The situation was not yet tragic, but it was certainly serious. With his usual foresight, Nguyen Ai Quoc realized that the opportunity he had been waiting for was being offered. The Japanese peril would give him (as it had given Mao Tse-tung in China) the possibility of uniting and mobilizing national energies and directing them to one sacred cause.

Therefore, at the end of January, 1941, Nguyen Ai Quoc finally returned to his native land after more than thirty years of absence despite the risks incurred by such a return. Prudently he remained near the Chinese frontier and took refuge in the calcareous caves of the Nung province, between Cao-bang and Tsin-tsi. From May 10 to May 19 he reunited there the principal representatives of the Indochinese Communist party as well as the responsible members of rebel groups—part pirates, part guerrillas—with whom the Vietnamese Nationalists had united. All of them had good reason to keep their distance from the French authorities.

The Nung province, with its topographical characteristics (nearly inaccessible caves and a frontier easily crossed when the French police were not too active) constituted an ideal refuge for these outlaws.

The Tsin-tsi Congress (a rustic meeting if ever there was one, with participants sitting on logs instead of chairs) brought about the creation of the *Viet-Nam Doc Lap Dong-Minh,* or *Vietminh,* and settled on the objectives of the program. The first objective was the struggle for independence against the Fascist powers, among which was the France of Vichy, which collaborated in Indochina with the Japanese and directed the movement under the sign *Cuu-Quoc,* National Welfare.

As Jean Lacouture has pointed out in his books, Nguyen Ai Quoc anticipated Moscow in this respect, for a few weeks later the Germans invaded Russia, and Soviet internationalism was supplanted by Russian nationalism. Nguyen Ai Quoc appealed to *all* Vietnamese, without distinction of class, religion, or political bias, in his famous "Letter from abroad," dated June 6, 1941:

> In past centuries when our country was in danger from the Mongol invasion, the old men of the time of the Thanh rose up. Our old men and our patriotic personalities should follow the example of those illustrious ancestors.

Did Nguyen Ai Quoc, as his Vietnamese biographers indicate, offer the French authorities in Indochina his collaboration in their struggle against the occupying Japanese? Probably not. He would have been taking too great a risk. Besides, one can hardly imagine the Indochinese Communist party joining the Fascists it had so strongly denounced. On the other hand, it is easy to predict how Admiral Decoux would have greeted such an offer from the revolutionaries he was pursuing.

From then on, the Indochinese Communist party regarded the Fascist Japanese army of occupation as its most significant enemy. Nguyen Ai Quoc stated this clearly in a keynote proclamation to the people. The partisans were to transform themselves into a resistance movement of liberation. Was this realism, opportunism, or patriotism? As usual, the motives of this man were complex, but one feels sure that patriotism was his prime motive. This idea is supported by what "Comrade" Ducroux said of Nguyen Ai Quoc many years after meeting him in Hong Kong in 1931: "A single thought occupies his mind and has, I believe, always obsessed him: the welfare of his native land, Vietnam. I won't deny that he was a sincere internationalist and true revolutionary, but Vietnam always took first place for him."*

During the months after the Tsin-tsi Congress, Nguyen Ai Quoc translated political books, sent out propaganda pamphlets and manuals of guerrilla warfare, and indoctrinated his followers. Already the two war chiefs of the Vietminh, the famous Vo Nguyen Giap and the montagnard Chu Van Tang, were attempting to instigate propaganda and intimidation operations aimed at the middle region, the Tonkin delta.

In July, 1942, Nguyen Ai Quoc decided to cross once again the frontier into China. It was a dangerous decision, but he needed to intensify his actions by obtaining the support of the Chinese Communist party, contacts with the party having become difficult. Perhaps he also hoped that Chiang Kaishek and his Kuomintang, in open war against the Japanese, might be induced to join him against the invader and furnish him arms and subsidies. According to some commentators, this was one of the reasons for his journey across the border. According to others, this reason was only a pretext. In any case, he understood the risks because he crossed the frontier disguised as a blind peasant and once more changed his

---

* Remarks made to Jean Lacouture and quoted in *Ho Chi Minh, his biography.*

name, at that time adopting a name with approprite Chinese assonance: Ho Chi Minh— "He who enlightens."

These precautions proved to insufficient. He had barely entered the territory when he was arrested. The fault, it is said, was that of his guide, a Chinese comrade who had been unable to show satisfactory identification papers at the check-point of the frontier.

For whatever reason, Ho Chi Minh, leader of the Vietminh, was imprisoned for fourteen months. Before obtaining the status of political prisoner, he was for many weeks dragged from prison to prison, his head immobilized in a cangue, his feet chained. He was linked to another prisoner, who eventually died at his side (no doubt he had been arrested at the same time as Ho). Weakened, his eyesight damaged, his body covered with scabs, Ho endured perhaps the hardest ordeal he had ever experienced. His faith and his culture° enabled him to withstand and surmount his torture, a fact that would amaze anyone not familiar with the quality of this man. Truly astounding is the way Ho Chi Minh turned this quasidesperate situation to his great political profit.

A story is told about this aspect of Ho, but his Vietnamese biographers pass over it rather gingerly. It can be assembled only bit by bit, but it is worth retelling. It should, however, be digested with the usual grain of salt.

The men upon whom Ho Chi Minh's fate depended at this time were the redoubtable Marshal Chiang Fa-kwei, governor of the Kuang-si province, and his right-hand man, General Siao Wen, expert in squelching subversion in Tonkin by utilizing some dubious but efficacious methods.

Chiang Fa-kwei, a typical warlord, speculated on the return of Tonkin under Chinese tutelage after the war. In order

---

° It was in these Chinese jails that Ho Chi Minh composed some of his best poems. Because he had no paper, he committed these verses to memory.

to promote his interests he had considered regrouping under his aegis the different Vietnamese Nationalists who had sought refuge in China, particularly in the frontier province of Kuang-si, by promising them support and supplies with which to resist the Japanese. Unfortunately the few Vietnamese leaders that Chiang Fa-kwei appointed to carry this out (among them was Nguyen Hai Than, of whom more will be said later) had remained in China for so long a time that they had become virtually Chinese. In addition, none of them had the prestige and authority required for organizing such a movement. Confronted with their incapacity, Chiang Fa-kwei began to look for another man.

When and how the imprisoned Ho Chi Minh informed his jailer that he was ready to be that man is not known. All that is known, according to this story, is that Ho proposed himself and that Chiang Fa-kwei accepted his offer. Was Chiang Fa-kwei unaware that the prisoner Ho Chi Minh was the Communist Nguyen Ai Quoc? Indeed, only a very few people were acquainted with the new name of Nguyen Ai Quoc. Even so, the story is hard to believe. Chiang Fa-kwei certainly had the means to be informed, and the fact that he had granted Ho Chi Minh the status of political prisoner indicates that he knew or at least had finally learned with whom he was dealing. Therefore, the version in which Ho Chi Minh persuaded Chiang Fa-kwei that no one in China or Indochina yet knew him by his new name (and thus his militant Communist background would not scare off the bourgeois Nationalists who were a part of the Vietnamese he hoped to regroup) is more likely.

What the conditions of the arrangement were is not known. It would be enlightening to discover them, but on this point, as on so many others, only Ho Chi Minh himself could have revealed them. All one can say is that Chiang

Fa-kwei and his henchman, General Siao Wen, were completely bamboozled. Ho Chi Minh, released from prison, was endowed not only with powers but also with subsidies originally intended for his rivals. Thus equipped, Ho Chi Minh hurried to put these benefits at the disposal of his partisans and to unify the Nationalist Vietnamese movements not to the benefit of the Chinese but to the benefit of his own aims.

A long period of political conflict followed, for Ho Chi Minh's associates were not so naive that they did not see through their colleague's scheme. Threatened with the loss of the authority they still possessed over their compatriots, they tried to employ other maneuvers. In an effort to pacify these compatriots and to make them see that they shared common objectives, Chiang Fa-kwei assembled a conference in March, 1944, at Laichau, bringing together the representatives of all the different Vietnamese Nationalist factions. A provisional government in exile was formed, in which the Vietminh was offered and subsequently accepted only one portfolio. Ho Chi Minh had realized the necessity of casting off ballast; he knew that by demanding more he would give his rivals an excuse to eliminate him.

As usual with Ho, he lost no time in theoretical discussions and in the quarrels that were his rivals' downfall. Ho Chi Minh continued quickly his revolutionary activities. His disciples worked at his side and intensified their propaganda in Vietnamese territory.

Events began to accelerate, and each day the goal to which he had dedicated his life loomed nearer, became more accessible.

The United States had entered World War II in 1941. Ho Chi Minh went to their headquarters at Kun-ming and obtained from the Americans the weapons and instructors he needed for the fight against the Japanese, who had by then become their common enemy. (It is even rumored that for a while Ho acted as interpreter at the American headquarters.)

Once again in his native land, Ho observed and directed the action of his young and impatient lieutenants—(Giap was in particular need of restraint) strongly advocating patience and moderation. Ho wrote and distributed a number of tracts, some of which reveal, in their prophetic aspect, a remarkable gift for political analysis.

Seeking an approach to Hanoi, his ultimate objective, Ho settled himself in a concealed strategic post of the Communist party's secret resistance movement. This was in the Thainguyen region, which was to be his refuge during the most crucial years of the revolution.

This extensive activity came to the attention of the French authorities, who ordered the military command to put an end to it by making a clean sweep of the mountainous region that was the traditional refuge of rebels and agitators.

On March 9, 1945, three days before the date set for this operation, the Japanese carried out a sudden attack on the fragile edifice of Admiral Decoux's French defense and toppled it. The military repression foundered, as did French authority. This wrecked a colonial enterprise that had been in existence for eighty years and that, despite its detractors, remains one of the glories of French civilizing action in the world.

From that time forward, nothing stood in the way of Ho Chi Minh's attainment of his goals. He was to profit immeasurably by this period of anarchy, which he had foreseen as early as September, 1944, in a tract that announced, six months before it occurred, the Japanese attack and the fall of the French Fascists. In this tract he added: "We will not even need to seize power since there will be no power to seize. . . . ."

However, there was a Vietnamese power, that of Emperor Bao-Dai, who, taking advantage of favorable circumstances, had denounced unilaterally on March 11 all past treaties with the French protectorate and decreed the independence of his country. But it was an independence supported by the Japanese and blemished with "collaborationism" of the most glaring kind. On the other hand, the authority of Bao-Dai extended only to the big cities, and he found himself confronted with economic problems almost impossible to resolve. The famine of 1944–1945 exasperated the populace and advanced the cause of the Vietminh, whose agents in Tonkin seized stocks of rice ((at least those that the Japanese had not thrown into the river)) in order to distribute them to the famished people.

It is true that French power no longer existed, but there were nevertheless some Frenchmen, isolated or in small groups, who attempted to resist the Japanese or who, on the Chinese-Tonkin frontier, waited to stage a comeback ((I was among the latter group)).

Ho Chi Minh approached these Frenchmen. His political acumen led him to think that Japanese fascism constituted the only objective upon which the concerted attacks of the Vietminh and the Allies ((British, American, Chinese, and French)) could converge.

It was thus that Ho sought, during that spring of 1945, the cooperation of and a union with the groups of French resistance fighters who were by then openly opposing the Japanese invaders. Thus it was that in July he sent a message to me in Kun-ming in which he stated five points, the basis of a future Franco-Vietnamese cohabitation, and made an effort to meet me personally.

5

FIRST CONTACTS

IN April, 1944, I was in London, conferring with the Free French officers shortly before the Allied landings in Normandy. In the course of my conversation with Colonel Passy and Manuel, his deputy, who was the head of the clandestine D.G.E.R.,* the subject of Indochina came up. They both knew that I was well acquainted with Indochina and they asked me if, after the liberation of Paris, I would be willing to transfer to the Far East and engage in an activity similar to my assignment during the German occupation of France. That is to say, in Indochina I would coordinate the underground resistance networks that had been established against the Japanese. I agreed to the proposition

---

* The initials stand for *Direction générale des études et recherches* the clandestine services of information and action of the Free French.

immediately, but events intervened that necessitated the postponement of the plan. News reached us that the Gestapo's latest operation had been against the resistance network in France, with disastrous results. I returned hurriedly to Paris. Then came the Allied landing, my arrest the following day, my escape, and the eventual liberation of Paris. These events covered several months and caused me to lose sight of the perspective of going to Indochina.

It was almost a year later—after the Japanese attack on Indochina in March, 1945—when I was still with the First Army, that I was recalled to Paris and the proposal of service in Indochina was introduced again. My status remained that of a volunteer, and my voyage out was arranged quickly.

Since the Japanese had dismantled the French resistance in Indochina, the mission that Colonal Passy had originally proposed to me, to establish liaison between various resistance groups, no longer had any meaning. What he now demanded was that I take charge of the French military mission in China, based at Kun-ming, the most important city in the southern province of Yunnan.

The work assigned to this mission was to gather all possible information regarding what was happening in Indochina, concentrating on Tonkin, North Annam, and Laos. To this end, commando troops were scattered along the Chinese-Tonkin border; the troops were composed of men, among whom were some native Indochinese, with a thorough knowledge of the region. The information gleaned from them was expected to be useful to the Allies, who were preparing a general attack against the Japanese forces. For the French these investigations would also reveal the temper of the Vietnamese and give France information regarding the activities of the Nationalist movements. And finally, we tried to learn the fate of our compatriots who had remained in Indochina under the rule of the Japanese.*

It is scarcely necessary to state that France had a particular interest in what our American allies called, with evident sympathy, the Vietminh League. Moreover, the Americans had acted as intermediaries and toward the end of July, 1945, had enabled us to receive the famous five-point message from the Vietminh, indicating to the provisional French government the amendments that should be made in any new constitution of French Indochina. These demands seem ridiculously mild today and did so even at the time, regardless of our hopes and illusions. But since Paris had neglected to inform us of the government's viewpoint, it was impossible to act officially; all we could do was to acknowledge receipt of the letter, signifying to our honorable American intermediaries that our own first reaction was favorable.**

Clearly we should see in this letter a first effort of Ho Chi Minh to dispel any fears we French might have had of him and of the movement he inspired and led. It was at exactly this time that the Americans, who were dealing with the Vietminh League, informed me that Ho Chi Minh would like to have a talk with me. The future President of the Democratic Republic of Vietnam very probably had heard of my

---

* For more details on this period, see the author's *Histoire d'une paix manquée,* 2nd edition, Fayard, 1967.

** The five points of the message were: (1) election by universal suffrage of a parliament to be presided over by the French governor until independence is achieved; (2) independence to be granted Vietnam within a minimum of five years and a maximum of ten years; (3) return of the natural resources of the country to its inhabitants, with indemnities paid to the colonials and economic concessions to France; (4) granting to the Indochinese of all the freedoms set forth in the United Nations charter; and (5) interdiction of the sale of opium.

talk with Nguyen Tong Tam in Kun-ming at the end of July. Nguyen Tong Tam was one of the ultra-Nationalist leaders in the Viet-Nam Quoc Dan Dang association (usually referred to simply as the V.N.Q.D.D.). Ho Chi Minh probably was afraid that Nguyen Tong Tam, not content with the already acquired Chinese support, was trying to insinuate himself with "new France" and that this meeting would save him from having the ground cut from under his feet.

It should not be forgotten that the Vietnamese Nationalists still had no clear notion as to what plans new France had for its big Asian colony. However, they did know the qualms the French had about the former Vichy régime and about some of the men who had represented that régime in Indochina. They also knew that many of us had fought against the Nazi occupation of France, and they correctly assumed that our ordeals in the underground resistance must have notably altered our concept of the future relationship of the capital to its overseas possessions. The declaration of March 24, in which the French government of General de Gaulle announced the idea of an Indochinese Federation composed of five states endowed with a certain autonomy (Tonkin, Annam, Cochin China, Laos, and Cambodia), had satisfied none of the Vietnamese leaders, for it took no account of the *de facto* independence Vietnam had acquired since the Japanese attack. In addition, it maintained and reinforced the division of the "three *Ky*" (the Vietnamese countries that constituted the old Empire of Annam, which all Nationalists hoped to see reunified).

I had not hesitated to tell Nguyen Tong Tam that although we would not let ourselves be forced to give concessions, we still remained faithful to the spirit of Brazzaville. In other words, France was ready to work out with the Indochinese themselves reasonable land leases and other agreements warranted by the circumstances and the political maturity of its protégés. Although my first reaction had been to accept Ho Chi Minh's proposal of a meeting at once, either in Kunming or in the region of Cao-bang, the meeting did not materialize. The tropical rains that inundate Yunnan and the upper Tonkin region had been the cause of the delay. Our first meeting did not take place until October 15, considerably later, perhaps too late.

If Ho Chi Minh had realized France's liberal intentions, would he have prevented the odious excesses committed when, a few weeks later, he ordered the uprising and seized power? It is doubtful. Such excesses are always manifested by an excited populace in similar circumstances. In any case, Ho was not completely in control of the situation, and while perhaps he deplored the terrorist acts, he may have felt that a climate of terror was indispensable to the ultimate acquisition of power. For that reason I regret that our conversations could not take place before the Japanese capitulation, but it is to be doubted that such an effort at a détente would have modified to any great extent the events that followed.

Perhaps the main difficulty was that the new government in France showed little interest in resuming control of Indochina. There was certainly a lack of clear instructions, and there was the problem of how to send new troops to reinforce those that Japan had reduced to ineffectiveness. Wartime conditions still existed. The few seagoing vessels remaining in control of France had been placed in the Allied pool and could not be employed without the consent of the Allies.

We who had been sent to represent France and to negotiate for her were thus compelled to adopt a vague attitude, not sufficient to convince the Nationalists of the futility of resorting to armed violence.

At any rate, the Americans who accompanied Ho Chi

Minh to the location in which our meeting was to have taken place informed me later that Ho seemed really to have wanted the French flag to be associated with the demonstrations planned for that occasion. This seems to illustrate the most characteristic concern of Ho Chi Minh—to placate.

The American liaison agents went so far as to assert that, in their opinion, the leaders of the Vietminh League had intended to make their entrance into Hanoi in company with the representatives of the provisional government of France. It is easy to imagine how Ho Chi Minh would have exploited the support of France after having obtained similar support and help from the Americans.

On August 6 and 9 the Americans dropped the atomic bombs that annihilated Hiroshima and Nagasaki. This hastened events to such an extent that it is a waste of time to speculate about what would have happened *if*.

On August 10, the day following the annihilation of Nagasaki, Ho Chi Minh, after transforming his guerrillas into the Army of Liberation of Vietnam, called for general insurrection; on August 13 he constituted a National Committee of Liberation. In Annam and Cochin China, as in Tonkin, Vietminh committees began to seek control of the towns and rural districts.

On August 14 the Japanese demanded an armistice. Two days later twenty thousand Vietnam demonstrators began to invade the Place du Théâtre in Hanoi, and for the first time the red flag with a gold star, the Vietminh flag, was flown in the capital. Eventually it would be the flag of the Democratic Republic of Vietnam.

The demonstrations on August 17 and 18 reached such a pitch that the imperial delegate, Pham Ke Touai, yielded power to a provisional leading committee. It is easy to surmise who were the leaders of that group.

On August 20 Tonkin was in the hands of the Vietminh. On the following day the Emperor Bao-Dai, called upon to abdicate, stepped down and became Citizen Thuy. The Democratic Republic of Vietnam was proclaimed, and Hanoi was named its capital, thus replacing the ancient imperial city of Hué.

Meanwhile, at Kun-ming I received the following telegram, forwarded by our mission in Calcutta:

G.P.R.F. [Provisional Government of the French Republic] caught off guard by the capitulation of Japan; count on us to provide against the worst pressures.

I had already reached a decision on August 9: I would go to Hanoi.

My plane landed August 22 after some preposterous mishaps; I traveled with a few of my colleagues on our mission, known as Mission 5. The Americans had grudgingly loaned us the plane, and we traveled under the guard of a group of Americans headed by Major Patti.

For the next few weeks, as I have recounted elsewhere [in *Histoire d'une paix manquée*], we lived dangerously. We were isolated in a tumultuous city, in which the tiniest spark could ignite a conflagration, and we were confronting the Japanese, who, though vanquished, still behaved like conquerors. Lacking the necessary power and authority—including an official title—I had nothing to depend on but chance and the devotion of my colleagues. Added to all the difficulties was the fact that the Americans who had accompanied me to Hanoi obviously wished I were elsewhere. Major Patti, for instance, was a rabid anticolonialist, and he regarded with a jaundiced eye anything that remotely resembled a return of French colonialism in Indochina. I was "bluffing" when I settled into the Palace of the General Government, as I had done before to console the French who had remained in Hanoi, and to make an impression on the Vietnamese Nationalists.

My first contact with the Vietminh was arranged by Major Patti. On August 27 he brought along two members of the provisional government of the Democratic Republic of Vietnam: Duong Duc Hien, Minister of Education, and Vo Nguyen Giap, at that time Minister of the Interior. Giap said he had been ordered to make contact with the first envoy of the Provisional Government of France. He added that he and his colleagues would be glad to receive "advice and directives." I knew that Giap, the erstwhile guerrilla, was one of the most brilliant products of our French schools, a distinguished graduate of our universities, a doctor of law, an accomplished pianist, and altogether a gifted man. He impressed me as being extraordinarily intelligent, steady, and strict. But at that time, according to the rule in Asia, our relations were courteously formal.

I told Giap and his colleague that I would wait to see what they accomplished before judging if they were worthy to hold command posts in the new Indochina and that they could prove their power and ability by putting an end to the disorders.

During this interview I announced to Giap, who appeared to be ignorant of the fact and was very upset, that according to the terms concluded without France at Potsdam, the Chinese army had been responsible for disarming the Japanese in the part of Indochina north of the 16th parallel. Therefore, after having endured the Japanese occupation, Vietnam would have to endure a Chinese occupation of Tonkin, North Annam, and a portion of Laos. The reaction of the future conqueror at Dienbienphu confirmed that the age-old fear of China was still very much alive in Vietnam.

The first Chinese troops arrived in Hanoi on September 9. Their presence furthered the prevalent disorder, and in

Tonkin great anxiety reigned. With suppressed fury I had to hand over to the Chinese "allies" the government palace that I had managed to hold out against the Japanese enemies.

While the Chinese exploited Tonkin to the hilt, the Vietminh intensified their propaganda and increased their provocations and their acts of violence against the French.

A week earlier, on September 2, Ho Chi Minh had made his first public appearance on the dais erected at Place Puginier. The occasion was the celebration of independence from the French. It was only then that the population discovered that their new leader was none other than Nguyen Ai Quoc, the famous revolutionary.

For our part, we had learned on September 7 that the second armored car division, headed by General Leclerc, was going to be sent to Indochina. On September 8 we at last had our first contact with the *Haut-Commissariat* of France in Indochina, in the form of a telegram from Governor-General Admiral Thierry d'Argenlieu, who had just installed himself in Chandernagor while waiting orders to move to Saigon.

Facing the deterioration of the situation (we had information that made us fear the worst), at the end of September I went to Chandernagor to put the facts before Admiral Thierry d'Argenlieu. After explaining the complexity and gravity of the situation in Tonkin, I asked to be replaced in Hanoi by an official representative of France. After all, I was only a reserve officer, and I owed my post in Tonkin only to the tragic misadventures of Pierre Messmer, administrator of the colonies, who had originally been selected to occupy it; he had been unable to arrive in time at Hanoi, having been captured and held prisoner by the Vietminh.

The admiral did not agree to my proposal. On the contrary, he asked me to continue officially the task I had begun unofficially and to return to Hanoi, where he would delegate his powers to me.

As I left his office, I passed through the office of his chief
aide. A blue-eyed officer was there, and he gave me an in-
tense look; then he exclaimed in surprise:

"Well! So this is the Jean Sainteny I've heard so much
about! I'm delighted to make your acquaintance. But it
seems you want to give up your post and abandon us to our
fate! And from all I've heard, this is very little like you. . . ."

It was General Leclerc.

I left for Hanoi with the title of *Commissaire de la République* for Tonkin and North Annam. Fortunately I had been
assigned some new collaborators and had been given supplies and necessary medicines.

During my absence from Hanoi, General Allessandri, military delegate for North Indochina, and Léon Pignon, his
political adviser, had made contact with Ho Chi Minh, whom
they described in a telegram sent to Chandernagor as "a
strong and honorable personality."

Upon my return to Hanoi, I too had conversations with
other Vietnam leaders, notably Nguyen Hai Than, chief of
the Dong Minh Hoi, whom we had already met in 1943 at
Kuang-si when he was disputing the power of Ho Chi Minh.

These encounters were disappointing. In the time that had
passed the two rival Nationalist parties had united, and Emperor Bao-Dai continued to evade my attempts to meet him.

Thus everything brought me back to Ho Chi Minh. He was
the one I had to see, the one with whom I must discuss the
situation.

6

DIALOGUES WITH
HO CHI MINH

F<small>ROM</small> the time of our very first meeting, October 15, 1945, I acquired, as had General Allessandri and Léon Pignon, the conviction that Ho Chi Minh was a personality of the first class. I knew that he would not take long to reach the forefront of the Asiatic scene.

At first sight there was nothing exceptional in his appearance. Of medium height, rather short in fact, thin, and seemingly fragile, there was something about him that was secretive and shy. Contrary to what his Vietnamese biographers say, his hair had not turned white in the Chinese prisons; it was still brownish, as was his goatee, which, with his high and bulging forehead, made him look more like the typical Annamese scholars one sees in the Latin Quarter of Paris than a fighting chief or a party leader. His most striking features were his eyes—lively, alert, and burning with extraor-

51

dinary fervor; all of his energy seemed to be concentrated in those eyes. As for the rest, he was usually dressed in the uniform now attributed to Mao, but Ho's uniform was rather shabby, and the tunic was rarely buttoned up to the neck. On his feet he wore the Yunnan cord-soled canvas slippers, and his socks always more or less sagged down over his ankles. Obviously he paid no attention whatsoever to his appearance.

Ho Chi Minh and I agreed to hold our interviews in private, without the knowledge of either the Vietnamese or the French population, not wanting to add to the prevailing tension. Thus it was at night that I left the Bank of Indochina building, where I had taken an apartment after being evicted from Government House by the Chinese, and went by automobile to the villa where Ho was expecting me. In the subsequent meetings the meeting place was usually a villa on the Paul-Bert public square. We did not know where Ho resided; probably he was not settled anywhere but frequently changed his residence. He was usually accompanied by Hoang Minh Giam, now Minister of Culture in North Vietnam. I was often accompanied by Léon Pignon.

These interviews continued over a period of six months. The object of our discussions was important and delicate. My job was to persuade Ho Chi Minh to agree to the return to Tonkin of the French troops, which would supplant the Chinese troops. It was, of course, futile to expect any restoration of French sovereignty in Indochina before being reinstated in Hanoi, the administrative and spiritual capital of the Indochinese Union and the nerve center of this turbulent peninsula. There was no possibility of bringing in an army, as in the former colonial style. The French units would have met with opposition not only from the hostile Vietnamese Nationalists, who were organized for guerrilla warfare, but also from the two hundred thousand Chinese troops that had swooped down on Tonkin with the intention of settling permanently if possible. There was also another group of adversaries to fear: thirty thousand Japanese. Theoretically the Japanese were being held prisoners, but their disarmament by the Chinese was being effected with a slowness that, although typically Oriental, was nonetheless disquieting. In addition to these impediments we faced the threat of a general encirclement of the delta and the provinces of North Annam, which would imperil still more the already precarious existence of the thirty thousand remaining Frenchmen.

It may be useful to recall that the problem was different in the southern part of the country, from which the Chinese were absent. That portion had fallen to the British at the Potsdam conference, and it was Great Britain's responsibility to disarm the Japanese army stationed south of the 16th parallel. They were carrying out this task loyally, and we were confident that we could depend on their support. Governor Cédille, who was Commissaire of the French Republic for Cochin China, had experienced as many troubles in the beginning as I was experiencing in Hanoi, but he was now officially established in Saigon, with the prerogatives attached to his functions. Likewise established there, no less officially, was Haut-Commissaire Thierry d'Argenlieu and, since the first week of October, General Leclerc, who was waiting impatiently to take his expeditionary corps north to Tonkin. The expeditionary corps was light, being comprised of only about eight thousand men, but the men, some of whom had served in the prestigious 2nd Armored Division, were courageous and experienced.

To prepare this operation we would have to establish not only a Franco-Chinese accord that would sanction the retreat of the Chinese troops (this was finally signed February 28,

1946, at Chung-King by General Crépin) but also a Franco-Vietnamese accord by which the Vietminh would agree to the return of French troops to the territory controlled almost entirely by the Vietnamese. Obviously this accord would make official the presence in Hanoi of a worrisome government, but that government was less to be feared on the spot and carrying out negotiations than retrenched in the mountain regions and waging a guerrilla war against the French.

General Leclerc had understood this very soon, as may be seen by the brilliant report he addressed to Paris on March 27, 1946, in which he repeated the anxieties I myself had mentioned in my own report at the end of December, 1945. I had concluded my statement with: "If it is probable that China will abstain from an armed conflict with France, her irregular units will give their entire support to the revolutionary Annamese troops across the frontiers, whose permeability is well known. Thus, if we attempt to reinstate the French government in Tonkin by force of arms, we must be prepared to meet with powerful resistance."

After four years of war and privation had France the desire and the means to launch into such an adventure? Obviously not; I had been convinced of this when I had been in Paris in July.

But why should Ho Chi Minh agree to negotiate, opposing the advice of those "ultras" close to him?

First of all there were political reasons. He was doubtless the strongest of the Vietnamese leaders, but he had rivals: the two Nationalist groups, Dong Minh Hoi and the well-organized Vietnamese Nationalist party, the Vietnam Quoc Dan Dang (V.N.Q.D.D.). These rivals manifested such hostility that it occasionally led to armed conflict in the frontier provinces. The doughty General Siao Wen, whom we had met in Kuang-si in 1942, had not lost hope of bringing

Tonkin within the Chinese orbit, especially now that two hundred thousand of his compatriots occupied the country. He himself had just arrived in Hanoi in the Yunnan military transport and was doing everything to carry out his plans.

It is clear—and this has been stressed—that Ho Chi Minh could not eliminate the Chinese menace without French support. On this point our interests coincided.*

Ho was also well aware that in order to construct, or reconstruct, the Vietnam of his dreams he needed the assistance of a great nation. That nation could not be China since China backed his adversaries. (It must not be forgotten that China at this time was not yet Communist. Mao Tse-tung would have to surmount many obstacles before becoming the ruler, and at this period he was confined to the north of China; he could do nothing for Ho Chi Minh.) Then what other country could assist him? Russia? Russia was still suffering terribly from the German occupation, and she too had postwar problems to solve. Then, too, Russia was turning all her efforts toward eastern Europe, which she was about to absorb.**

Moreover, Ho Chi Minh was far too patriotic to play the game of some members of his party, former militants of the Indochinese Communist party, which was eager to include Vietnam among the satellite republics of the U.S.S.R.

---

* Some Vietnamese, in turn, berated the French for negotiating with the Vietminh in the hope of getting help in ridding the country of the Chinese menace. According to this accusation, we had no intention of respecting our promises once the peril had been removed.

** However, it seems that a Russian mission was being sent to Hanoi at this time—a mission that never arrived. Perhaps Chiang Kai-shek had put too many obstacles in the way or had managed to prevent its departure from Moscow. We must also bear in mind that Stalin's Russia and Chiang Kai-shek's China were Allied powers in the war against the Axis powers.

France was another possibility. The intellectuals of Vietnam possessed the language and culture of France, which would facilitate cooperation. Ho Chi Minh certainly had more affinities with France than with any other nation. In 1945 France was no longer a conquered nation, at least not in Europe, and in France the Communist party was expanding, members of the party having acceded to power in the new administration.

Ho Chi Minh had always been a realist. His political strategy of advancing by one landing stage after another had been defined in his five-point message sent to me in Kunming, and he seemed to believe that this was the best means to achieve the total independence of his country. Why not avoid, then, the wasteful expenditures of a war if he could do so by negotiating?

In addition to this political strategy Ho had the subtle Oriental mind that could find satisfaction in being able to treat on equal terms the representatives of the tutelary power he had for years secretly fought. This man who had all his life combated French imperialism now envisioned with a certain pride the idea of being the first to bring to the barely sketched edifice of "French Union" the Vietnamese keystone.

According to Jean Lacouture, Ho may also have believed that in agreeing to a negotiated settlement he would facilitate the decolonialization of other French possessions in Asia and Africa. Quite possibly this may have been the case. Ho Chi Minh had considered the colonial problem in its entirety ever since the years of his youth, when he argued in *Paria* for the emancipation of "all oppressed peoples."

Some commentators have gone so far as to speak of pacifism. One does not know what to think about this suggestion. Certainly Ho Chi Minh sought at this time to convince us of his dislike of violence. No doubt it would not have displeased him to be regarded as the Gandhi of Indochina. One part of him admired that great example, but Ho Chi Minh, although nurtured on the teachings of Confucius, had none of the religious or philosophical motives of a Gandhi that would make him abstain from resorting to violence. He did not oppose the use of violence within his country and against his compatriots. For example, it was certainly not without his approval that the Vietminh, later, decided to eliminate some of their rivals, the pro-Chinese Nationalists, and did so in the most radical way. On this and other such occasions Ho Chi Minh and his seconds claimed that they acted only in self-defense. But their methods were as brutal as those of their adversaries.

We must take care not to simplify in depicting Ho Chi Minh's personality. Niether pacifist nor fire-eater, he no doubt was revolted by certain solutions that contradicted his nature and the personality he was carefully shaping. But when his schemes, his companions, or he himself was threatened, he did not hesitate to adopt violent methods. In this respect he belonged entirely to that Asia so rich in contradictions, where the most refined torture follows the most exquisite courtesy.

To attain his goals with us Ho Chi Minh was clever enough not to be as exigent as were some of his rivals. While his rivals demanded total and immediate independence as a condition of any negotiation, Ho Chi Minh declared that he understood quite well that he could not attain what he wanted immediately and that he would be content with relative independence, accepting a gentleman's agreement with France that would bring about, after a lapse of time, the total independence of his country. Why should we suspect him of insincerity? He had waited thirty-five years, and he could wait a few more years. Patience is an Oriental virtue.

Not that our talks were easy! Ho Chi Minh argued each phrase, word by word, in our tentative accords. While he argued he smoked continually—Chinese cigarettes, American cigarettes, or the strong Gauloise cigarettes. Pignon smoked even more, and I pulled on my pipe. Our talks ended late at night in an atmosphere as thick with smoke as an opium den—without the euphoria. Although our talks were conducted in French, I often felt we were not speaking the same language. How many times as we left these sessions my aides and I felt that we would never reach an agreement! Ho Chi Minh often asked for time to reflect or to consult his friends and counselors, often "his" private counselor.

That privileged counselor was Vinh Thuy, the former Emperor Bao-Dai.

The relations Ho Chi Minh maintained with his former emperor during this period demonstrated fully his adroit style of maneuvering. In truth he was playing such a subtle game with Bao-Dai that I often felt he scarcely understood it himself. Bao-Dai was introduced in a variety of ways: as supreme counselor of the new government; as the future constitutional monarch of the establishment Ho and his friends were struggling to form; or as a citizen who had stepped down from the throne of his own accord, the better to aid the national revolution.

In this connection, I recall an amusing incident. One day during a session of the provisional government of the Democratic Republic of Vietnam a minister of Ho Chi Minh addressed Bao-Dai as "Counselor" and was reproved by his chief.

"You might address him as 'My Lord,' as I do," said Ho Chi Minh!

The importance of Bao-Dai's presence was that that the Vietnamese population, profoundly shaken by the recent upheaval, would be reassured by the participation of the traditional monarch in the new government. Bao-Dai was put on display at all the important meetings; he was associated with all the decisions made; and when, on March 6, 1946, after the signing of the Franco-Vietnamese Accords, I paid the formal visit to Ho Chi Minh required by State etiquette, the former emperor was at his side. A few hours later, when Ho Chi Minh paid me the no less formal visit, Bao-Dai accompanied him. When they witnessed the former leader in the company of the head of the provisional government being received by the French government, the crowds were licensed to think that, by his presence, Bao-Dai validated not only the seizure of power by Ho Chi Minh and his friends but also the entente just concluded with France— the protective power that, a few hours earlier, they had been exhorted to drive out of the country by any possible means.

When were those two men sincere in this association, labeled farcical by so many? Were they simultaneously sincere? Did Bao-Dai hope to save some small shred of legitimate power from the wreckage? Did he honestly desire to cooperate in the change taking place? This would appear to be the case if we are to judge by the content of his beautiful letter of August 20 to General de Gaulle and the wording of his abdication of August 25. However, uncertainties still remain. Was he sincere until the very moment when, realizing he had been duped into handing his people over to the Communists, he yielded to the Americans, who, in August, 1946, took him to Hong Kong aboard one of their planes? Or was his behavior that of a man playing for time and thinking only of escaping a fate he had good reason to fear?*

---

* We learned later that Bao-Dai was disturbed at this time by some complications in his private life; this might partially explain these uncertainties.

During this period of negotiations Ho Chi Minh no doubt became aware that I had tried in vain to meet Bao-Dai privately in order to find out his state of mind. At any rate, Ho contrived to persuade me that the former emperor was being kept informed of the development of our talks. One day he even went so far as to remark that if our negotiations were successful, I might have to conclude them "with someone else."

Some people believe that Ho Chi Minh actually considered maintaining Bao-Dai in power, but that, at the last moment, when the leader had done his job of acting as cat's paw, Ho decided to reap the benefits himself. I find it hard to believe. It is more likely that Ho Chi Minh used Bao-Dai just as long as he felt that he was essential to consolidate his own power and to allay the fears of the majority of his compatriots, who favored independence but were averse to obtaining it by adhering to Marxist doctrines, so little in harmony with the traditional structures of Vietnamese society.

As for the Americans, Ho Chi Minh had played the game of seduction with them so brilliantly that when he seized power, their delegates in Hanoi gave him their blessing. What a sad irony this is in the light of current events!

Still more astounding is the fact that Ho Chi Minh managed, during the period when he was about to seize power, to obtain the good will of the Japanese. When one recalls the Japanese hatred for communism and the power they still maintained over Indochina, one can only applaud Ho for performing a very clever trick. True, the Japanese, furious at having to abandon Indochina, may not have disliked the idea of leaving behind them this time bomb represented by a Communist Vietnam. Besides, at this point the Japanese may have felt that political color was less significant than racial color. Then, as now, "Asia must be left to the Asians!"

Thus, the Japanese would not have lost the war completely, as Marshal Teroki was later to declare.

It would be tedious to recount in detail the interminable conferences we had with Ho Chi Minh and his advisers before we reached a successful conclusion. The formula *Doc-lap*—"independence or liberty!"—was the obstacle most frequently encountered. (General Leclerc in Saigon—where he assumed the interim government of Governor-General d'Argenlieu—whom I kept informed of developments in the negotiations, actually cabled Paris that independence might have to be pronounced.)

Another point of dispute was the future status of Cochin China. Ho Chi Minh wanted the territory to be officially integrated with the new Vietnamese state (the famous union of "the three *Ky*"). France wanted just the contrary. We argued that the Cochin Chinese people should decide their fate in a free election. These differences caused interruptions somtimes lasting several weeks, until a helpful intermediary brought the French and Vietnamese negotiators once more into contact. That intermediary was often Louis Caput, a French colonial of long experience, a member of the militant activist corps of the S.F.I.O., and a person highly trusted by Ho Chi Minh because Caput had formerly supported some of Ho's aspirations.

The formula accepted by Ho Chi Minh a few minutes before the signing of the preliminary agreements on March 6, 1946, was "A Free State in the Indochinese Federation of the French Union."

At several meetings preceding this signature I told him that the accords about to be sanctioned could be signed only by the head of a government that represented not only the Vietminh but all political parties of any standing in Vietnam.

As it happened, almost all the moderates had been eliminated for the benefit of the Vietminh in the government that had been constituted on November 3. Had my words been listened to or had Ho merely wanted to neutralize the opposition and make it share the responsibility of an entente with France? The answer to that question is impossible to determine, but the fact remains that the National Vietnam Assembly, which met March 2 in the municipal theater, included at least a hundred moderate deputies, and the government of national union that was designated on March 9 included only five out of eleven members of the Vietminh party. But Ho Chi Minh remained president.

Because of the tides the landing at Haiphong of Leclerc's expeditionary forces could not be made except between March 5 and 7. The accords, therefore, had to be signed between those dates; otherwise the operation would be an ill-timed demonstration of strength and might lead to serious problems.

On March 5 I received a letter written by Colonel Lecomte and forwarded by General Leclerc. In it I was informed that the Chinese, after agreeing to the landing, had recanted and, in violation of the agreements concluded with us at Chung-king or pretending not to know of them, refused to admit French troops into Indochinese territory, or at any rate to permit the landing until after the signing of a Franco-Vietnamese accord.

My instructions were to remedy this situation immediately, "even at the cost of initiatives that could eventually be disavowed." Then, on the night of March 5 the conference that seemed about to terminate happily fell into an impasse. Léon Pignon and I withdrew, asking Ho Chi Minh to think over the matter. I had made it clear to him that the next day would perhaps be too late; the warships transporting Leclerc and his troops were within view of the Tonkin coasts.

Shortly before dawn on March 6 Hoang Minh Giam came to my residence to announce that the president accepted my conditions. I had found an unexpected ally in the person of a Chinese officer, General Chao, who, more aware than his colleagues of the tragedy that an armed confrontation could precipitate, had taken the initiative of persuading Ho Chi Minh to reach an agreement with France. (It must be added that this Chinese general, like many others, was afraid that in the battles that might follow some of the booty the Chinese had accumulated would be lost before it could be embarked.)

Our vicissitudes were not yet over. Toward nine o'clock on the morning of March 6 I learned that a Chinese unit at Haiphong had opened fire on the French cruisers as they went up the river toward the port city. The worst was avoided only because the French, with admirable coolness and discipline, endured the murderous attack for twenty minutes before making a riposte.

Léon Pignon and I had our last talk with Ho Chi Minh before the signing of the accords shortly after noon, but the incident was not mentioned. Possibly Ho Chi Minh had not yet heard of the grievous incident. The radio-telegraphic connections to which he had access at the time were almost nonexistent, and those of the Chinese were little better. In any case, we experienced great anxiety until four thirty, the hour designated for the official signatures. Our anxiety was justified, for the citizens of Haiphong had already decked the city with flags celebrating "the Sino-Vietnamese victory over the French army."

At four o'clock the Vietnamese delegates appeared at the rendezvous, a villa in which we had often met with Ho Chi Minh. Before an audience that included some Allied observers, very satisfied with the outcome of the talks, the agreement was read aloud. Ho Chi Minh was first to sign; then he handed the pen to his Deputy-Commissaire of National Defense, Vu Hong Khanh.

When the ceremony was over, I expressed my satisfaction to Ho Chi Minh.

"And I," he replied, "am sorry, because fundamentally you have won the contest. You were well aware that I wanted more than this. But I realize well that we cannot have everything at once." Then, recovering his usual vivacity, he embraced Pignon and me, saying, "My consolation is our friendship." *

Ho Chi Minh instructed Vu Hong Khanh to sign after him probably because this colleague was a notorious Francophobe. In obtaining his endorsement, Ho Chi Minh perhaps thought he was providing against any propaganda that might accuse him of betraying the cause of independence.

However, this precaution was not enough. As soon as the accords were made known they were used against Ho Chi Minh by the various opposing factions (Nationalist, pro-Chinese, and pro-Moscow). The word *Viet-gian* ("traitor to the country") was soon circulating in the town. The old fox, people said, has been tricked by the French, who are protecting themselves behind fallacious promises; they'll take back their power over Indochina, their troops and tanks will be here in Hanoi within a few hours, and repressive measures will begin once more, worse than ever.

Upset by these rumors, Ho Chi Minh suggested to me that we post on the city walls a proclamation, signed by both of us, calling the public's attention to "the peaceful arrival" of French troops for the purpose of abetting the Franco-Viet-

---

* The accords of March 6 were completed on March 8 after the accessory agreements regarding military contingencies had been settled between General Salan and General Giap and signed by them.

namese accords that granted to Vietnam, now a free state, the right to form her own government and to administer independently her laws. Again because of his anxiety, Ho Chi Minh appeared on the balcony of the municipal theater early on March 7 to give explanations.

In this confrontation with the populace, which for long months had lived in a state of uncertainty and excitement, the fate of the Franco-Vietnamese entente that had been concluded the night before was settled; certainly the fate of the old revolutionary and his partisans was settled. It can be justly said that the people, ignorant as they usually are in such cases, greeted the accords with indifference; the opposition parties were aroused; and the activists seized upon the occasion to discredit and eliminate this devil of an old man who had checkmated them for much too long. Ho Chi Minh's opponents managed within a few hours to organize and agitate the crowd that had poured into the public square. Quite evidently the crowd wanted an accounting of what this man had done the night before when he signed the entente with the representatives of France, a protectorate nation that only a few days earlier they had been exhorted to expel.

On the theater balcony General Giap spoke first, promising the people to continue the fight that they seemed to want. He was acclaimed. By way of contrast, no doubt planned but effective all the same, Ho Chi Minh spoke next, merely explaining what had been done. The sincerity of his tone and the emotion that broke his voice, which was never strong, swayed and persuaded the crowd that had moments before been demanding an explanation. In this peroration, addressing not only his compatriots but the whole expectant world, Ho summed up his position and his politics.

In the course of this dramatic confrontation Ho Chi Minh was most thoroughly himself. He was an adroit speaker, who knew how to argue a point and how to acknowledge his weaknesses. He announced to his compatriots the sacrifices that must be made in the event of a war. He spoke in the same way as he was to address me a few weeks later in Paris, when he predicted the breakdown of our entente. ("Then we will fight each other," he said, "and you will kill ten of my men while I kill one of yours.")

His tone, his frankness, the fragility of his person, and the humility of his attitude were very persuasive. He did not attempt to impress or to intimidate. On the contrary, he emphasized the difficulties that had to be overcome—indeed he exaggerated them, which made him all the more convincing. The indomitable will that flashed in his eyes, illuminating his features, made one understand that he would not hesitate to do anything to achieve his goal when he added (as he would reiterate in Paris at the end of a verbalized meditation), "And in the long run, I will win!"

But to return to that month of March, 1946. Leclerc had been waiting twelve days to make his entry into Hanoi. Impatiently he paced the deck of his ship, tapping it with his legendary cane. Finally, on March 18, he brought in his troops. The rejoicing of the French populace, delivered from a five-year nightmare, remains one of my most thrilling memories.

In the late afternoon of that day I took Leclerc to meet Ho Chi Minh. I had already introduced him to General Vo Nguyen Giap, who had said, "The top resistant of Vietnam is pleased to meet the top French resistant." With Ho Chi Minh there was no reason to fear a similar breach of good manners. Besides, Lelerc managed with a smile and a few simple words to gain the sympathy of the old revolutionary, who was too sensitive not to admire the determination of the great army man and to perceive his forthrightness. We posed

The birthplace of President Ho Chi Minh. (*Photo, General Delegation of the Democratic Republic of North Vietnam.*)

Ho Chi Minh at the Congress of the Socialist party in Tours, 1920. (*Photo, Snark International.*)

Ho Chi Minh in about 1942.

Author Jean Sainteny and Ho Chi Minh enroute to Along Bay. Taken aboard the seaplane *Catalina* on March 24, 1946.

Aboard the *Emile Bertin* in Along Bay, March 24, 1946. From left to right: Ho Chi Minh, Jean Sainteny, General Leclerc, and Admiral Thierry d'Argenlieu. Back facing the camera: Nguyen Tong Tam, Minister of Foreign Affairs of the Democratic Republic of Vietnam.

Ho Chi Minh and Jean Sainteny after their meeting with Georges Bidault in July, 1946 (*Photo, Agence Intercontinentale.*)

President Ho Chi Minh in Paris, 1946. (*Photo, Albin-Guillot — Viollet.*)

Ho Chi Minh during the negotiations at Fontainebleau
in the summer of 1946.

After the breakdown of peace negotiations at Fontainebleau Ho Chi Minh took refuge in the jungle in order to lead the battle against the French forces.

From a secret command post Ho Chi Minh launched a war of harassment. Behind Ho is a photograph of Nikolai Lenin and Josef Stalin, his mentors.

Ho Chi Minh's arrival at the airport in Peking, June 25, 1955. At his right is Mao Tse Tung. (*Photo, Associated Press.*)

Ho Chi Minh observes the battle front in September, 1950. (*Photo, General Delegation of the Democratic Republic of North Vietnam.*)

General Delegate Jean Sainteny presents his credentials to President Ho Chi Minh and Pham Van Dong, December 16, 1954.

Ho Chi Minh
and General Giap.

Ho Chi Minh talks to the people. (*Photo, General Delegation of the Democratic Republic of North Vietnam.*)

Ho Chi Minh speaks at a public convocation. (*Photo, Dalmas.*)

The "good Uncle Ho" surrounded by children during a party held at his home in Hanoi. (*Photo, Associated Press.*)

President Ho Chi Minh and Prime Minister Pham Van Dong. (*Photo, Marc Riboud-Magnum.*)

Jean Sainteny is greeted by Pham Van Dong upon his arrival in Hanoi for the funeral of President Ho Chi Minh, September 8, 1969.

for the press photographers as we drank a toast to Franco-Vietnamese friendship. . . .

The most difficult matter still remained: to set up a meeting between Admiral Thierry d'Argenlieu and Ho. The admiral had expressed the desire for an official encounter with the president of the Vietnamese government who had signed, in my person, an accord with France. I arranged it, and he invited Ho Chi Minh aboard the cruiser *Emile-Bertin*, in the incomparable setting of the Along Bay, on March 24. A camera shot depicts Ho Chi Minh and me in the hydroplane *Catalina* as we flew out to the flagship. It shows me filling my pipe and the leader of the Vietminh sitting prosaically beside me, a tropical hat on his head, his hands folded over his bamboo cane. But his sidewise glance toward the photographer is fierce, the look of a hunted animal ready to spring. Was he afraid?

When I recollect, today, that we were in a military plane, with the enormous bulk of the cruiser looming ahead, a veritable floating fortress bristling with guns, I realize that he had needed courage to accept that interview and in doing so was giving France a rather splendid vote of confidence.

The meeting took place without mishap. On the deck of the *Emile-Bertin* honors were rendered Ho Chi Minh, who responded to the welcoming toast of the admiral very simply, without compromising himself.

That afternoon we broached the question of what should follow the accords signed on March 6, for these were only preliminary conventions, a foundation, one might say, on which to build. We settled down in the admiral's cabin to discuss this, and the admiral had the opportunity to observe the patience we had employed and the patience still needed to reach a satisfactory result with a person like Ho Chi Minh.

The place in which the preliminary conventions should be

drawn up in conclusive form was the first question. Admiral Thierry d'Argenlieu wanted the conference to be held in Indochina, where all the experts were gathered at the time, and he proposed the town of Dalat. Ho Chi Minh wanted the conference to be held in Paris—not only for reasons of prestige but also because he wanted the French people to witness the meeting and in a way to guarantee the validity of the accords. To deal with the admiral at Dalat would all too unhappily recall the colonial accords that had been signed in former times with other admirals-governors, whereas to be welcomed in Paris by the French government and to negotiate there was to be recognized as the head of an independent state. For several reasons General Leclerc and I also favored the idea of Paris as a meeting place. Mainly it would remove Ho Chi Minh from the pressures exerted on him by his entourage and by Chinese influence. But we also wanted to take ourselves out of the frenzied atmosphere, the "colonialist" atmosphere maintained in Tonkin by those who wistfully recalled the past.

It must be remembered that this attempt at a peaceful decolonialization was the first ever tried. The very word "decolonialize" had not yet even been coined. Regrettably but quite naturally the undertaking met with strong resistance in some quarters, often for honorable reasons but sometimes for reasons less than honorable.

And if Ho Chi Minh was being treated as a *Viet-gian* by some of his compatriots, I for my part was soon to be treated as a *bradeur d'empire,* a person who dismantles the empire and sells if off like junk.

7

IN FRANCE

When it was settled that the negotiations would be pursued in France, if not in Paris then at least in Fontainebleau, Ho Chi Minh must have felt a legitimate satisfaction. But with what apprehension it must have been mixed!

Many of his partisans thought he was committing a serious error in going to France. The risk of falling into a trap haunted their minds. Some of those who accompanied him to Paris confessed to me afterward that they had been afraid of being arrested, especially when it became clear that the Fontainebleau conference was going to fail. (The misfortunes incurred by the Sultan of Morocco and by Ben Bella, *a posteriori*, would seem to justify their fears.)

Although he had desired the meeting to the utmost, Ho Chi Minh probably wondered if he were not throwing himself deliberately into the lion's mouth by going to France.

But I believe that in Hanoi we managed to quiet his worst fears. He trusted us; would he likewise trust the authorities in the capital?

I wonder if France has ever appreciated the extent of the homage Ho Chi Minh paid the French by such trust. He agreed to travel to a country that still exercised protectorate powers over Indochina, a powerful nation that had pursued him for almost thirty years and had condemned him to death!

Of course, Ho Chi Minh had good friends in France. The extreme left had acceded to power at the end of World War II. Indeed, in the administration of Georges Bidault seven ministers were members of the Communist party, and six were Socialists. And this would be the administration that would welcome the President of the Democratic Republic of Vietnam.

But Ho Chi Minh was not unaware that some Frenchmen in the homeland, as in Indochina, did not approve of the political line that sought a new *modus vivendi* with former protégés of France who had rebelled against French authority. He knew that these laggards, although not in the majority, could influence the course of events, could inevitably turn to their own profit some incident or other, and could stir up the French troops in Indochina, temporarily superior in strength if not in number, making them restore the *statu quo ante bellum,* those prewar conditions to which they obstinately adhered.

Aside from his uncertainties regarding the kind of welcome he might receive in France and the results of the negotiations there was another anxiety for Ho: the excitable condition of the Vietnamese population, periodically swayed by all kinds of wild rumors.

I imagine that Ho kept a painful memory of the happenings of March 7 when he had employed all his cleverness in that speech delivered from the balcony of the municipal theater in Hanoi in order to convince the people that he had done the right thing in signing the preliminary accords with France. He knew that his enemies rejoiced at his absence. He also knew that the Chinese, for whom the Franco-Vietnamese accords meant the collapse of their traditional ambitions in regard to Tonkin, would certainly take advantage of his absence to attempt a reversal of the situation in favor of their puppets, the Nationalist parties.

For all these reasons it was only normal for Ho Chi Minh to instruct his aides, before he left Vietnam, to be "ready for any eventuality." It was this famous recommendation of May 31, 1946, that caused all the opponents of a peaceful settlement, no matter what their stripe, to label Ho Chi Minh a double-dealer. And that document seems even to have greatly troubled Leclerc himself.

I went to Paris ahead of Ho Chi Minh, in April, 1946, to make arrangements for his journey and to prepare the public and the French government for it. I wanted to explain the meaning and importance of the accords that had just been concluded and to show that these accords had rescued us from an abyss and had opened up certain desirable perspectives if we continued to play the game.

On April 25, at half past eight in the evening, I paid a visit to the vice-president of the Council of Ministers, who was then Maurice Thorez. He approved the terms of the March 6 accords. To my great astonishment, he had obviously studied the document thoroughly.

"The agreements are very satisfactory," he said, "and we have nothing to add or subtract. If the Vietnamese do not respect the terms, we will take the necessary measures and let guns speak for us, if need be."

In making that surprising statement Maurice Thorez may have had in mind only the pro-Chinese Nationalists, who one could not unreasonably suppose would be responsible for a possible rupture.

Escorted by General Salan, Ho Chi Minh boarded a plane for Paris on May 31.

And at this point there occurred another of those mishaps that shook the frail edifice of the entente. A government crisis intervened; the cabinet presided over by Félix Gouin had just been overturned when Ho arrived, and there was no one to give an official reception to the President of the Democratic Republic of Vietnam.

The two planes that were bringing Ho Chi Minh and his entourage had to be rerouted to Biarritz.

As soon as Georges Bidault was designated as the new premier he asked me to organize the entertainment for Ho Chi Minh during his stay in France. In the course of an interministerial meeting, which I attended, it was decided that Ho and I should remain out of the Fontainebleau negotiations in their initial phase, after which we could "take a hand in the game." Meanwhile, we must keep Ho Chi Minh satisfied until the government was able to welcome him.

I left at once for Biarritz.

Perhaps it was during his first stay on the Basque coast (from June 12 to June 22) that Ho Chi Minh proved his stamina and gave me reason to appreciate his self-control.

Waiting those ten days in idleness for a new French administration to be formed was not our only problem. There had also been some disquieting news from Cochin China. Anticipating the decisions that might be made at Fontainebleau, on June 1 Admiral Thierry d'Argenlieu had declared Cochin China an autonomous republic, and Ho Chi Minh heard the news on the radio while flying over the Middle East en route to Paris.

It should be recalled that unlike Annam and Tonkin, territorial protectorates of France, Cochin China was a French *colony*. This fact, added to the desire of a segment of the southern people to retain their autonomy and their mistrust of the Democratic Republic of Vietnam, will explain why the admiral wanted to assure this particular destiny for Cochin China.

But for Ho Chi Minh, whose supreme goal was to unite under his rule "the three *Ky*"—the three countries that formerly constituted the Annam Empire—this was a distasteful measure in every respect. It was an attack on the territorial integrity of Vietnam. It was an underhanded blow that made him doubt the good intentions of the French. And in Hanoi the opposition was saying that we had taken their president out of the country in order to dupe him. They were comparing Cochin China to Alsace-Lorraine.

Even in France, before Ho Chi Minh's arrival there were certain Vietnamese elements who took him to task. The announcement of his journey had given rise to a published "Letter to Comrade Nguyen Ai Quoc," which attacked him in these terms:

> You have signed an agreement accepting autonomy for Vietnam, not its independence. To the extent that we had faith in you when your name stood for great revolutionary thought, we are now full of anger and ashamed at having chosen you as our leader. . . . You have backslid, you have betrayed your own ideas. . . . You are betraying the grandiose destiny of the Vietnamese people. . . .

This letter concludes with a hope and a threat:

We are inclined to believe that the Vietnamese are only temporarily hopeless. Sooner or later the struggle you have been unable to carry on to the finish will be continued. . . .*

No sooner did he disembark from the plane at Parme-Biarritz than Ho Chi Minh actually proposed returning at once to Tonkin. He was nervous and reticent. I reassured him as best I could by telling him that the decision regarding Cochin China was temporary and in no way prejudicial to the referendum provided for in the accords of March 6.

He did not mention the subject again. Concealing his bitterness and impatience, he applied himself readily to everything we planned for his diversion. Everyone who spoke with him during that forced holiday was struck by his good humor and simplicity. In short, he behaved as if he was on a carefree vacation, not at all like the head of state anxious to open and discuss the all-important dossiers he had brought with him.

Several times I took him to Hendaye, where my sister had a villa. Ho Chi Minh spent some time with my nephews on the beach, seeming really to enjoy watching the youngsters playing and enjoying themselves. He was at this time, literally, "the good Uncle Ho."

In the small village of Biristou, where we went several times, he was the perfect tourist, interested in everything, wanting to understand everything he saw. In the visitors' book at the inn where we had our lunch he wrote: "Seas and

---

* Although this letter was signed, there is reason to think that Ho Chi Minh may have written it himself in order to make the French aware of the concessions to which he had agreed. I myself suspected this. On the other hand, had this been so, the letter would surely have been distributed more widely than it was.

oceans do not separate brothers who love each other."* The statement is still there.

One day we embarked before dawn on a tuna fish trawler at Saint Jean-de-Luz. The fishing was good, but the day on the sea in the turbulent Bay of Biscay seemed long. The crew, not knowing of the past seagoing experiences of the President of the Democratic Republic of Vietnam, were amazed at his stance on deck and his total freedom from sea-sickness. Ho Chi Minh singlehandedly caught several tuna and seemed to be enjoying himself thoroughly. He charmed everyone with his easy manner and ready wit. I recall the captain's mentioning the Basque Separatist movement and how at once Ho commented: "In that field I am certainly more experienced than you are, sir, and I would emphatically urge the Basques to think it over very carefully before taking the plunge!"

In later years Ho Chi Minh liked to recall these days on the Basque coast, which, he said, provided him with some of the happiest memories of his life.

We finally left Biarritz for Paris on June 22. The weather was fine, and since we were running a little ahead of schedule, I instructed the pilot to make a slight detour in order to give our guest a view of the châteaux of the Loire. This unexpected tourist trip reminded me of the countless training flights I had made for aerial reconnaissance over those same châteaux in 1939, when I was a novice in the air force. As we flew over Tours, Ho may have been reminded of how, still a young man, he had witnessed there in 1920 the birth of the

---

* Someone has flippantly added after Ho Chi Minh's signature: "Gone with the wind." If the writer meant to say that the signature would be erased by the wind of history, he was wrong. Until his death Ho Chi Minh remained at the head of a country that had confronted France and is continuing to hold out against a super-power.

French Communist party and how the party chief, Marcel Cachin, had given him his first opportunity to make a public speech. . . .

At four o'clock we were over Paris. The Bourget airport was thick with crowds of people. Marius Moutet, Minister of Colonies, was there, surrounded by numerous distinguished civilians and military notables representing the French government. Above the airport floated the associated flags of France and Vietnam.

Glancing at Ho, I observed that he was deathly pale. His eyes glittered, and when he tried to speak to me, his throat was so tight that he could not utter a word. As the plane stopped on the runway, he grasped my arm.

"Stay close to me," he said. "There's such a crowd!"

And suddenly I saw before me "the young Indochinese" of the 1920s, for his timidity had been noticeable at the Congress of Tours when Marcel Cachin gave him the chance to speak and again in Paris when the truculent Léo Poldès had showed him off at the Club du Faubourg. He was timid, yes, like a night bird suddenly exposed to bright light, but he was intelligent enough and possessed enough willpower to regain control by the time we emerged on the landing platform. By that time we had passed the point of no return, and he knew that no matter what happened, he had to play his part. He did so with amazing poise.

He had returned to France, against whose authority he had ceaselessly fought with all his strength for almost thirty years, as a chief of state, and he was being given an official welcome according to the most rigid protocol. Such a situation demands of the man placed in it an unusual amount of tact and finesse.

Once again Ho Chi Minh's innate simplicity enabled him to pass this new test. Far from trying to assimilate the usages of state etiquette, which he had never before had to consider, far from patterning his behavior on that of the notables surrounding him, he remained himself. He readily allowed Jacques Dumaine, director of protocol in foreign affairs, to guide him. In an agony over Ho's complete ignorance in these matters, Dumaine tried to teach him the essential notions of diplomatic practice, but Ho Chi Minh, while submitting to this instruction, still maintained his characteristic disarmingly ingenuous manner.

With smiling indifference he accepted the suite of rooms reserved for him at the Royal-Monceau hotel on the Avenue Hoche. I knew that he would find the beds in that hotel too luxuriously soft and would prefer to sleep on the wall-to-wall carpeting in his bedroom.

I do not believe that he was making a bold show of power when he issued his early-breakfast invitations that soon became famous. He would say to someone who wanted to be granted an audience, "Why, of course. Will you have breakfast with me tomorrow morning at six o'clock?" One rises early in the tropics.

Ho Chi Minh remained imperturbably faithful to his usual way of dressing: canvas sandals and a straight tunic, now buttoned up to the neck as a slight concession. He nonetheless respected the social practices of others. On the engraved invitations to the large dinner he gave on July 4 at the Royal-Monceau hotel in honor of Premier Georges Bidault he included the direction "white tie." But at that dinner he remained faithful to the costume he made famous long before Mao.*

---

* Ho Chi Minh was not unconscious of his picturesque appearance. A tremendous crowd of people assembled to watch the procession that escorted him up the Champs Elysées to lay a wreath on the tomb of the unknown soldier. Someone in his entourage commented: "Well, Your Excellency, you certainly have drawn a crowd of people!" "Why, of course." Ho replied with a burst of laughter. "Everyone wants to see the Vietnamese version of Charlie Chaplin!"

From his former stays in Paris he retained a fondness for the city and its people. He enjoyed going about *incognito*, mingling with the passersby, revisiting the places where he had lived, worked, and conspired. . . .

For example, he asked me to go with him to see the film about the wartime resistance engaged in by railroad work- ers—*La Bataille du rail*, it was called—and it was, I believe, the only film that dealt with the subject of the recent war at that time. Contrary to what some people said, he did not want to see such things "to pick up ideas," for conditions of the resistance in France were very different from conditions in Vietnam. No, it was not for this reason, which would have betrayed the efforts of the French and the Vietnamese to find a *modus vivendi*. He wanted to see the film merely because he felt great sympathy for the struggle that the French peo- ple had waged against the Nazi occupiers of their country.

No doubt it was in the same spirit that Ho Chi Minh asked to visit the coast of Normandy where the Allies had landed. On the short drive there an accident occurred that permitted me to assess once more the extraordinary self-control of this man.

I had just left my car to join Ho Chi Minh in his when we saw it suddenly veer off the road and overturn in a ditch with its occupants, our aides.

The idea that an attempt on his life had been made came to Ho Chi Minh, as it came to me. However, he let nothing of this feeling show, and he shared in the efforts we made to rescue our friends from the overturned car. Fortunately they were hurt only slightly. The car, on the other hand, was ut- terly wrecked—much to my dismay since the car, a Buick, had been the property of the Japanese commander-in-chief of North Vietnam, and General Leclerc had given it to me.

After we had arrived in Normandy, I offered Ho Chi Minh the use of a farm I owned there. When I woke up next morning rather early I was thrown into a panic when I learned that my guest had disappeared! He was eventually found strolling in the fields. He had risen at dawn and had visited every nook and corner of the property—chicken yard, stables, everywhere. He had admired the livestock and had chatted with the resident farmer, who had explained our methods of breeding cattle and other aspects of farming to him.

During the interministerial conference that had been arranged for Ho Chi Minh's stay in France it had been agreed that all contacts between him and the French government should be made through me. Respected at first, this order was to become dangerously relaxed later on, for Ho Chi Minh often went over my head to obtain what I felt, with good reason, should be denied. Most of the time I was informed of his displacements and his encounters. No doubt some of them were concealed from me, but I believe this happened rarely. Besides, if I were not informed by Ho Chi Minh himself or by one of his aides, I was informed by our special services. Although Ho played the game it is clear that many members of his suite were more circumspect in their activities and the contacts they were determined to make.

No sooner had we arrived in Biarritz than the major part of the Vietnamese delegation that had accompanied us disappeared in the direction of Paris, in spite of the fact that they had declared their desire to be at their president's side during his official reception by the French government. Many of them were Vietnamese citizens who resided in France and had volunteered their services. But they began to engage in all kinds of political activities; this was especially true of the Vietnamese delegates entrusted with the negotiations soon to take place in Fontainebleau.

Thus Ho Chi Minh was allowed to play the part he wanted

while his compatriots took care of creating the climate, preparing the ground that would be favorable to their ambitions when their representatives at the conference would state them.

As is well known, they did this with considerable maladroitness and virulence, spurred on by the French of the extreme left, who, during this period, were throwing oil on the fire of discontent. They compromised, whether intentionally or not, any chance of reaching a peaceful settlement at the conference.

Their behavior was illogical and shortsighted since they had unreservedly approved the preliminary accords of March 6. The intransigence to which they drove the Vietnamese negotiators contributed to the inevitable occurrence of what they were soon calling "the dirty war." A more moderate and realistic attitude might not have prevented the breakdown at Fontainebleau, but in any case it would have disabused the Vietnamese of the dangerous idea that a part of French opinion was ready to support their war of independence if events obliged them to resort to violence.

It was in this spirit that Charles Tillon, the Minister of Air in the Gouin cabinet, accompanied by some friends, could not resist paying his ridiculous surprise visit to Biarritz. He went with the object, he said, of "noting with my own eyes in what conditions Ho Chi Minh and his suite are being held in Biarritz." He himself must have realized how laughable was his visit when he saw Ho Chi Minh installed at the Carlton, the best hotel in Biarritz at that time, where everything was being done for the comfort of the Vietnamese chief of state, the official guest of France. The hospitality extended to Ho Chi Minh was his right, and he expressed his pleasure in it.

Ho Chi Minh's stay in Paris caused a variety of reactions, as can be imagined. Many businessmen, politicians, and journalists were impelled by sheer curiosity to make the acquaintance of this mysterious personage, whose fantastic existence was beginning to become known. Assailed by demands for audiences, I decided to give a reception to which I invited everyone who desired to meet our distinguished guest.

The reception was held at my Paris town house, where the garden in the month of July offered agreeable possibilities. Many politicians of various rank were present, and they clustered enthusiastically around Ho. When I introduced Albert Sarraut, former governor-general of Indochina and the declared enemy of the old revolutionary, Ho was greatly amused by the greeting of his ex-enemy.

"Well!" exclaimed Sarraut, "here you are, you old brigand. I have you within reach at last! What a good part of my life I've spent pursuing you!"

The old revolutionary often recalled the remark, always adding an expression of esteem for the former governor-general and minister of the colonies.

Ho Chi Minh appeared to be sincerely touched by the welcome we gave him, but he was profoundly disappointed because he was not able to meet General de Gaulle, who had only recently retired to Colombey after leaving power and, as he was to do later, in April, 1969, had made it a rule not to intervene in affairs of state. One of Ho Chi Minh's greatest desires was to meet the leader of the Free French forces, whom he so greatly admired. Several times he asked me to arrange a meeting, and when he discovered that it was impossible, he entrusted to me the traditional gift of one head of state to another, his voice and eyes expressing regret as he asked me to give it to the general.

He was also upset by Leclerc's sudden change of attitude. The two men I had brought together in Hanoi after the signing of the March 6 accords were obviously drawn to each other, but during the four months that Ho Chi Minh spent in France Leclerc avoided Ho. Leclerc's frequent absences from Paris were not sufficient to explain his evasiveness. The break became obvious when Leclerc refused even to attend the garden party at Bagatelle, which was given to permit Ho Chi Minh to repay his social obligations.

Ho felt acutely this double frustration, and he felt repudiated. I cannot affirm it without some hesitation, but I suspect that being slighted by the two great men of the Free French forces led him to think that France's attitude had changed. This increased his mistrust of the French and darkened the atmosphere of the last days he spent in France. *

---

* Leclerc had been severely criticized by some of his peers for his "liberal" action in Indochina. Because of this he obviously did not want to meddle further in Indochinese affairs. Georgette Elgey published in her *République des illusions* a letter from Leclerc to Maurice Schumann, dated June 8, 1946, in which he states that he had proof, through intercepted documents, of Ho Chi Minh's deceitfulness. This letter was quoted by Georges Bidault in two magazine articles (*L'Aurore* and *Minute*) on the occasion of Ho Chi Minh's funeral ceremonies, and I believe Leclerc was referring mainly to the letter from Ho to his disciples, dated May 31, just before his departure to France, stating that they should "be ready for any eventuality." Then again, in 1967 General Valluy's article in the *Revue des Deux Mondes* also alluded to intercepted Vietnamese documents that could have impelled the high command in Saigon to take a harder line. For the sake of history, I hope these documents will one day be made public and the debate resolved.

8

BREAKDOWN OF THE PEACE NEGOTIATIONS

ALMOST everything has been said that needs to be said about the breakdown of the Fontainebleau peace negotiations. Perhaps France should have chosen a top-ranking political figure to head the French negotiators. It seems, too, that we should have set up a precise agenda, as did Pierre Mendès-France in 1954 at Geneva, in order to curtail the Asiatic dilatoriness.

French political passions were overheated at the time, and this too was a factor in the eventual breakdown of negotiations. While the Communists fervently supported the Vietnamese revindications, the conservatives, in reaction to this, encouraged the French negotiators to stand firm and screamed "treason!" at anyone who gave in to Vietnamese demands. As a result, tensions increased from day to day, hour to hour, and disbelief in a satisfactory outcome infected both camps. Not much was required to intensify the usual mistrust of the Vietnamese, who were always inclined to believe that all France wanted was to circumvent the accords of March 6.

But these questions of form or climate would not have been enough to torpedo the conference had there not been some nearly insoluble fundamental differences of viewpoint.

The main disagreements involved the union of "the three *Ky*," the custom house duties, diplomatic representation, the place to be given the French language. In reality the Democratic Republic of Vietnam wanted to obtain all the prerogatives of an independent state, but France wanted only to recognize the prerogatives of an autonomous state. As has been stated before, Ho agreed to the French Union and repudiated Federation, which divided Vietnam.

The breakdown was already easily predictable when the news reached Paris that a "federal" conference had been called precipitately for August 1 at Dalat by Admiral Thierry d'Argenlieu; the purpose of the conference was to determine the position to be given not only to Cambodia and Laos in the Indochinese Federation but also to Cochin China, thus indicating that France definitely wanted to exclude those nations from the Democratic Republic of Vietnam.

This action brought about the immediate suspension of the negotiations, but because of Ho Chi Minh's intervention we managed to resume them a few days later. However, in both parties to the conference faith was destroyed.

At the beginning of September the Vietnamese delegation, headed by Pham Van Dong, banged the door shut and embarked for Tonkin.

But Ho Chi Minh stayed on.

When his official stay in France came to an end, the administration made it clear to Ho that he could no longer stay as the guest of the French government at the Royal-Monceau hotel. This position, logical and conforming to practice, added its weight to the more or less discreet pressure being exerted on the president of the Vietnamese republic to make him return to his homeland. But Ho Chi Minh did not leave. Instead, he invited himself to Soisy-sous-Montmorency to be the guest of the Raymond Aubracs, a couple who had shown much admiration and sympathy for him during his official stay in Paris.*

The leader of the Vietminh ended his stay in France as a guest in that private home. There he received numerous visitors, who usually found the old revolutionary in the garden of the Aubrac villa, sitting on the grass or on a big flagstone and responding willingly to the interviews sought by journalists and others.

The post-Fontainebleau period had begun. But did there remain a chance for a period of grace, a chance that armed conflict might be avoided? The continued presence in France of Ho Chi Minh seemed to indicate that there was indeed such a chance. But war loomed ahead, for the situation in Indochina continued to disintegrate after Ho's departure.

Repeated incidents tried the patience of the French, even the Frenchmen who refused to admit that armed conflict was inevitable. In the month of June attacks on civilians and military began. An attack likewise was made against Commander Simpson-Jones, chief of the British mission in Hanoi, who was generally regarded with esteem by the French and the Vietnamese alike. (This attack was a flagrant example of the

---

* Raymond Aubrac along with Professor Markovitch, was to play a part as mediator in the conferences of 1967, which gave rise to the peace conference of Paris at which Americans and Vietnamese argued once again the question of the eventual cessation of hostilities.

tactic that specialized in victimizing "the good whites," many
of whom had already been victims before I arrived in Tonkin—physicians, nuns, people who had devoted their lives
to improving the conditions of the native population. On the
other hand, the rare specimens of rabid colonialism had more
or less been spared.)

A French convoy was attacked on the road to Bac-ninh
on August 4. Was the attack made by uncontrollable Vietminh elements (with hindsight, it would appear to have
been) or by pro-Chinese elements? Regardless of blame,
twelve French soldiers were killed and others wounded. The
anniversaries of the days of August, 1945, when the Vietminh
had seized power, were marked by anti-French demonstrations, which, while merely verbal, were nonetheless ominous
and in contradiction with the aims of the French-Vietnamese
efforts for a peaceful settlement that were being made at
Fontainebleau.

I told Ho Chi Minh quite firmly that it was up to him, even
at a distance, to put an end to these excesses, which risked
defeating our efforts in the past year to bring about a close
cooperation within the framework of internal autonomy, prefiguring eventual independence.

Most of these incidents had obviously been meticulously
prepared. I told Ho this in a number of tense conversations,
but he refused to agree with my interpretation.

I was right, but Ho Chi Minh's responsibility cannot be
ascertained. Along with other questions it is still too clouded
over to be answered conclusively. I still think, as I thought at
the time, that it would have been illogical for Ho Chi Minh
to take the initiative in this systematic destruction of the
détente he and I had succeeded in creating. Indeed, what
had he to gain by it? Surely the entente was necessary to the
accomplishment of his plans, which no longer required a war
in order to be realized.

Besides, although the Fontainebleau conference had failed, Ho Chi Minh's stay in France had been a success. His personality had conquered many who had previously had their doubts or had been outright adversaries. His methods of persuasion and his charm had made him "a one-man show"; he had succeeded beyond his own expectations. Why, then, would he destroy the fruit of his efforts? He was much too shrewd not to see that every new hostile incident chilled the ardor of his most sincere well-wishers, destroyed the most lively sympathies, and had a disastrous effect on public opinion, to which he was very sensitive.*

When I mentioned my worries about the deterioration of the political climate in Hanoi and asked Ho to return there and put an end to the incidents, he replied that he understood my viewpoint quite well but that if he returned "emptyhanded," he would be discredited and consequently powerless.

"Don't let me leave France like this," he said one day in the presence of Marius Moutet, minister of colonies. "Arm me against those who are trying to outstrip me; you'll have no reason to regret it."

I think he was sincere, but his attitude seemed to prove to others his duplicity, his Machiavellianism. And the skeptics said, "He is now trying to get through blackmail what he was unable to get through negotiation!" Yes, they said, he wants to be given certain advantages that will enable him to disarm his enemies—who are also our enemies—or at any rate to restore his friends' confidence in him so that he can retain their

---

* Ho Chi Minh would surely have heard of what French Communist party head Maurice Thorez had declared: "Guns will have to speak for us." He must have realized that other Frenchmen would not recoil from that eventuality. Thus, if he had believed even for a moment that harassment might serve his purpose, he would soon have realized he was on the wrong track.

help in making his enemies see reason. The demonstration
of authority he could thus give became all the more convincing with each violent incident. . . .

Worse, his detractors went on, Ho Chi Minh was pretending that he wanted us to arm him against his opposition, but
he would certainly employ those same arms against us eventually.* These detractors concluded that if Ho Chi Minh
were not a master of duplicity, he was a pitiful sorcerer's apprentice and in any case not to be trusted.

This interpretation of his behavior troubled many people,
perhaps Leclerc himself. I have given much thought to this,
asked myself many questions, but for all the reasons I have
enumerated I continue to think that the hypothesis of Ho Chi
Minh's premeditated and permanent duplicity during this
period is unacceptable.

If he had been double-dealing, why would he have asked
me on September 2 to send a telegram to Hanoi requesting
that the ceremonies commemorating Vietnamese independence be stripped of any character inimical to France? Did
this action not indicate that eventually he hoped his representatives would be associated with France? And why was
he so eager to sign with Marius Moutet that pathetic *modus
vivendi* of September 14, a paper hastily drawn up in my
office, giving him so much less than he had hoped for when
he came to France?

That he realized to what extent his hopes had been
cheated is supported by something he said in a low voice as
he was borne away in a motor car. I did not hear him say it,
but others did: "I have just signed my death warrant."

---

* Following our preliminary accords of March 6, the accords of
March 8 provided that the Vietnamese tactical units would be in-
corporated into our troops and equipped by them. Since the Fontainebleau conference failed, the Vietnamese were left without arms except
those they already possessed.

At a luncheon I gave in my home before the signing of that lamentable paper, I did hear him make another significant remark. It was after he had once again implored Marius Moutet in vain to give him arms against his enemies.

"Then," he said resignedly, "if we must fight, we will fight. You will kill ten of my men while we will kill one of yours. But you will be the ones to end up exhausted."

As a matter of fact, this eventuality had never left his mind, and he now realized that if he was not returning to Hanoi completely emptyhanded, he was still not taking back what was needed to appease his aroused compatriots.

It must be remembered that at this time Ho Chi Minh did not have the power and prestige that were to be conferred on him later by his victory over us. Nor was he the only master of the game. The bellicose Giap, who was acquiring increasing authority, believed far more in war than in peaceful settlements; he considered conferences useless postponements. In this respect Giap resembled most military men. Certainly Ho Chi Minh's colleagues had allowed him to attempt a solution by negotiation because he knew France and the French and because he was the only one who could engage in talks with us with any chance of success. Did they ever really believe in a successful outcome? There had been no successful outcome, and they were now desperate to obtain by more ruthless and more efficacious means what they wanted: the independence of a unified Vietnam.

Having signed the *modus vivendi*, Ho Chi Minh decided to return to Tonkin, though he did so regretfully. Yet what more could he expect? That he had stayed on in France in the hope of obtaining more from us can easily be understood, but his behavior at that point is hard to explain. He wanted to return to Vietnam by the slowest possible means even though the circumstances demanded his speedy return. . . .

He refused to take the plane that was put at his disposal. He gave reasons of health as his excuse. He wanted to return by boat, and when I was unwilling to cooperate in this, he went directly to the minister of the marine and was given passage on the *Dumont d'Urville*, which was soon to leave for Indochina.

This determination of his to travel over water is the only really disturbing factor. Was he afraid of an attempt of his life, which could be carried out more easily in the air than at sea? But whom did he suspect of fomenting such a thing? Or did he hope that the irreparable would take place in Indochina while he was still abroad? Did he know that an irreparable incident was going to occur, and did he not want to prevent it? This is possible because it was only two months later, on December 19, that the general uprising took place.

I accompanied Ho Chi Minh as far as Toulon. At Montélimar our railway coach was surrounded by a crowd of Vietnamese. With my permission, he addressed his compatriots, explaining why he had signed the *modus vivendi* and asking them to work hard at their studies without occupying themselves with politics, which he would handle. The same thing occurred at Marseilles, where a few shouts of *"Viet-gian!"* ("Traitor!") were heard in the crowd. But these shouts were made by a few Frenchmen, elected Communists of the town who brought this anti-French note to the meeting, exhorting the Vietnamese to struggle to the end against "French colonial oppression."

The next day, on September 19, on the deck of the *Dumont d'Urville*, I bade goodbye to Ho Chi Minh, thinking I would never see him again.

All I wanted at that time was to rest and to attend to my personal affairs, which had been neglected during these years spent in the service of my country; but there was no one who wanted to take my place in that service, which had become less and less attractive. General Morlière, who was deputizing for me in Hanoi, had a great deal to do, for the situation was worsening from day to day.

Upon his arrival at Haiphong on October 21, Ho Chi Minh tried to take the helm once more. When he disembarked, he spoke to the assembled crowd and tried to pacify it. At Hanoi he went further, managing to persuade the welcoming crowd to sing the "Marseillaise" after the Vietnamese hymn. That was perhaps his ultimate pro-French demonstration.

For a while longer the old fighter tried to carry out his policy and methods, but on November 11 an incident showed that a breakdown of the structure was imminent. At the last moment Giap canceled Vietnamese participation in the ceremonies arranged to commemorate the armistice of 1918. The French troops paraded alone in Hanoi.

But what lit the powder fuse was a question of custom house duties. On November 20 a Chinese junk carrying a cargo of contraband gasoline was seized by the French navy in the port of Haiphong. Only six days earlier the Vietnamese assembly, following Vietminh instructions, had demanded that the French government should respect "the sovereignty of Vietnam over matters pertaining to custom house duties." While one of our boats towed the junk toward the Haiphong harbor, some *tu-ve* Vietnamese* opened fire on our marines. Our marines vigorously returned the fire. A rapid accord was concluded between Vietnam Minister of the Interior Nam and our French director of political affairs, Lami. There was reason to hope that the incident would have no adverse aftermath. But on November 22, judging that events had reached

---

* The *tu-ve* were members of "self-defense" groups and were drawn essentially from among youthful Vietminh militants.

a climax, the office of the haut-commissaire of Saigon, in the person of General Valluy (who was deputizing for Admiral d'Argenlieu, at the time absent on a mission to Paris), ordered the commander of the reserve forces of Haiphong to seize power and establish order there.

The operation, supported by artillery, was harsh. There may not have been twenty thousand dead, as the Vietnamese claimed, but very likely there were several thousand. It is unnecessary to describe the effect produced by this affair upon the native population, particularly as exploited by the extremists. Hanoi, drilled with underground galleries, was already prepared for street fighting.

The French government had not waited for this critical incident to order me back to Tonkin as fast as possible. Appointed governor with plenipotentiary powers, both civil and military, I left Orly on November 23 and arrived in Saigon on November 26. There, General Valluy (still deputizing for Admiral d'Argenlieu) asked me to wait until the operations in Haiphong had ended before taking up my post in Hanoi.

As a matter of fact, the Haiphong operation had ended, but Valluy had strict instructions from the admiral, and, as he told me later, he did not want to risk compromising me by involving me in military incidents, since I was the only negotiator left. Then, too, after an absence of close to seven months I needed time, so he said, to familiarize myself with the situation in Tonkin.*

I did not arrive in Hanoi until December 2. Before leaving Saigon I had been given a *Note d'Orientation* from the haut-commissaire. It read as follows:

---

* Although I was in Saigon six days, General Valluy did not deem it necessary to communicate to me those famous "intercepted documents" that had enlightened him as to the duplicity of the Vietminh and had incited him to set in motion the Haiphong operation.

Military honor having been saved, French prestige restored and enhanced, it would be a mistaken policy to impose unduly harsh conditions.

Henceforth it is essential not to go too far in forcing Ho Chi Minh and his government to take desperate measures. For this reason I consider as premature and inopportune your installation in the palace of the general government, for it will be interpreted as a deliberate provocation signifying the return to forceful methods. . . .

When my plane landed on the Gia-lam airstrip, all the French and Vietnamese notables were there to welcome me—except Ho Chi Minh. Giap apologized, saying that Ho was ill and confined to his bedroom. Nonetheless I considered the absence of the president a bad omen. A few months earlier Ho Chi Minh would have been the first to welcome me.

With increasing anxiety I took note of the almost desperate situation. Both French and foreign observers told me that only the confidential relations that had been established between Ho Chi Minh and me could stave off the worst. Naturally I asked to see him at once. The faithful Hoang Minh Giam, who had been our intermediary in March, confirmed that he was indeed ill but that he would see me as soon as his condition permitted.

On December 3 I was brought a letter from Ho Chi Minh:

I will be very glad to talk with you here this afternoon between five and six o'clock. Because of my present state of ill health it is understood that our visit together will be a visit between old friends. . . .

I found Ho Chi Minh in bed. His eyes were glittering and his hands, which held mine for a long time, were hot with fever. Hoang Minh Giam and Nam, who were in attendance upon him, did not leave the room, and he did not ask them to leave so that we could be alone together. We spoke of the usual banalities: his health, my plane trip, and so on. Finally he alluded to the events in Haiphong, which had deeply affected him, and he hinted that those events were not alien to the illness that obliged him to remain in bed.

"You see," I told him, "I was right to be worried in Paris about your prolonged absence from your country."

"That's true," he replied, "but you too were a long time in returning."

Our conversation ended there, and in the following days it was with Hoang Minh Giam that I tried to find a way to bring about an easing of the situation and a return to mutual confidence. Giam kept his chief informed of our conversations. When I expressed astonishment at having found, upon my return, all the moderate elements in the Vietnamese government eliminated to the benefit of some notorious Francophobes, Giam asked me, "in behalf of Ho Chi Minh," to name the men I deemed undesirable. A sequence of events gave me no time to do this. I often wonder if I would have done so even if I had had the time.

Acts of violence and assassinations were becoming frequent occurrences. Barricades were thrown up in the streets overnight. Either out of fear or on orders, a part of the native population fled Hanoi, which almost resembled a desert. In the delta the situation was no better, and when I made a tour of inspection, my low-flying plane was machine gunned several times.

Ho Chi Minh had again begun to receive several Western

visitors, but now his actions were surrounded by mystery. We began to wonder about just how much freedom of action he retained.

On December 11 I received a letter from him; that is to say, he sent me an appeal to the Assembly and the French government. The document was unsigned. I sent the document back to him and asked him to initial it. Despite the urgency I waited several days before the signed document was returned.

If only I could have had precise instructions from Paris, but none came. Alas, once more France was without a government.

On December 12 the Socialist Léon Blum returned to power. On December 15 Ho Chi Minh addressed a message to him that was delayed "in transmission" at Saigon and did not reach Paris until December 26. Thus there was nothing for me and General Morlière to do but to prepare for the worst while keeping open the possibility of negotiations.

But our talks with Hoang Minh Giam, General Giap, and Nam, led to no détente. On the contrary, our interlocutors unanimously blamed the French for the acts of violence. In note after note and talk after talk, the tone became more shrill. Early on December 19 I sent the following letter to Ho Chi Minh on my official stationery as Commissaire (or Delegate) of the French Republic to Tonkin and North Annam. I reproduce it here:

To: M. The President of the Government of the Democratic Republic of Vietnam

Sir:

I acknowledge receipt of a special letter from Monsieur Nam, Delegate of the National Defense of Vietnam,

dated December 16, reminding me that I am "the pro-
moter of the accords of March 6" and making "an urgent
appeal" to my "political acumen."

It reaches me simultaneously with the detailed account of the incidents that occurred in Hanoi on the
17th inst. Thus I learn of a violent attack on a supply
truck delivering food supplies as it passed down the Rue
Jambert. The occupants of the truck were killed. This
veritable massacre was immediately punished, as such
incidents of aggression would have been in the past had
I not trusted your government utterly.

I also learn that two French civilians have been hei-
nously attacked in their homes by a band of armed
hoodlums. One of the civilians was killed; the other, a
young girl was gravely wounded.

This outrage, which, in any well run country, would
have been punished, may remain unpunished, as have
many preceding ones.

This act of violence was committed by men belong-
ing to a paramilitary formation that, if not controlled
directly by our government, nonetheless acts with your
government's authority.

In his letter to me Monsieur Nam deplores "A re-
crudescence of incidents due to elements of the French
army." That is debatable, as you know, and once more
I reject the accusation. But the heinous crimes that we
deplore are undoubtedly committed by elements recognized as being under the authority of the Vietnamese
government. Consequently I am obliged to bring to your
notice the following:

I must expect of the Vietnamese government that it
will see to it that the perpetrators of this unjustifiable

outrage committed upon defenseless civilians are found, arrested, and punished within twenty-four hours after the receipt of this letter.

Once that delay is passed, I must again regret the laxity or the ill will of your police services and shall assume the right to take personally all the steps needed to find the culprits and avoid the repetition of crimes that, to quote the words of Monsieur Nam, "are far from coinciding with the spirit of the Convention."

Yours respectfully, [etc.]

Circumstances being what they were, I am not sure that Ho Chi Minh ever received my letter. On the other hand, by a strange coincidence, I received a letter from him early in the morning of that same day, December 19. In it he asked me to meet immediately with Hoang Minh Giam in order "to find with him a solution for ameliorating the political atmosphere." I notified him that I would expect Giam in the course of the following morning, December 20, but I was never to know what Ho Chi Minh wanted to say to me. As far as I was concerned there was no December 20.

For several days the rumor had circulated that the Vietminh was getting ready for a general attack, but there had often been rumors of the kind. Then, when the Yersin hospital clock, quite near my office, began to strike eight o'clock, I said to my colleagues, "Apparently it's not for tonight. I'm going home."

Scarcely was I in my car when I heard the rumble of a muffled explosion, and the town was instantly plunged in darkness. The power station had been hit. The time was four minutes past eight o'clock. Exactly at the same hour on March 20, 1945, the Japanese had initiated their attack on

Indochina. Perpetual students, the Vietnamese were putting into practice the lesson the Japanese had taught them.*

I managed to reach my home, and there I jumped into a machine gun carrier General Morlière had sent to convey me to the fort, as we had arranged in case of the expected uprising. I did not go far. In the Avenue Borgnis-Desbordes the car passed over a mine: a deafening roar, increased by the sound of the explosion of grenades nearby. One of them set fire to another vehicle carrying ammunitions. . . .

How I managed, wounded as I was, to get out of the blazing car and to survive during the next two hours is a mystery, for I spent them sprawled on the pavement surrounded by my dying comrades. I knew only one thing: the Indochinese war had begun. And in the darkness, ripped open by flashes of gunfire, all our efforts and hopes were swallowed up.

In the hospital I had no news from Ho Chi Minh, and when I returned to work for a brief period at the government residence, I still had not heard from him. The fate of the people was in the hands of the military.

About four months later, after I had returned to Paris, I was surprised to receive a letter from Ho Chi Minh. I will quote it in its entirety, for it is perhaps the strangest letter he ever wrote to me. It is dated February 24, 1947, and it normally should have reached me before my departure from Indochina. I still ask myself what caused the delay.

Here is the letter, which was written on the official stationery of the Democratic Republic of Vietnam:

---

* Those same Japanese had not as yet totally evacuated Vietnam, as is evidenced by the fact that certain of their cadres had taken part in the December 19 attack on Hanoi.

To: Monsieur Sainteny
   Delegate of the French Republic
Dear Friend,

I have just learned that you are returning to France. I send to you and Madame Sainteny my best wishes for a safe journey and good health.

I am sure that, like me, you profoundly regret that our common efforts to bring about peace is demolished by this fratricidal war. I know you well enough to tell you that you are not responsible for this policy of force and reconquest.

That is why I want to repeat that, in spite of what has happened, you and I remain friends. And I can also declare to you that our two peoples also remain friends.

There has been enough of death and destruction! What should we do now, you and I? France has only to recognize the independence and unity of Vietnam for hostilities to cease immediately, and once peace and confidence are restored, you and I can then get to work on the reconstruction, for the common good of our two countries.

For my part I am ready to work for peace, a just and honorable peace for our two countries. I hope that you, for your part, will work toward the same end.

May God accord us success!

Devotedly yours,
Ho Chi Minh

This ultimate appeal for peace, this astonishing reference to God, this *satisfecit* he awards me, forgetting his own responsibilities and those of his friends, provide surprising material for amateur psychologists. Once more the question arises of Ho Chi Minh's sincerity. Did he really mean it when he stated that nothing more was needed than for France to recognize the "independence and unity of Vietnam" for the fighting to cease, after which the Vietnamese would cooperate?

These are superfluous questions. Even if we had so desired, we could not have granted what he demanded. In reality there was no Indochinese policy in Paris. How could there have been, with a political system that toppled an administration after an average of only three months of existence?

For a long time, however, the most clear-thinking Frenchmen occupying important posts in the capital and abroad had comprehended the determination of the Vietnamese and knew that they would never renounce their efforts to obtain their independence. As represented by those men, France also recognized the justice of the Vietnamese aspirations. The maturity of the Vietnamese, the astonishing facility with which they had assimilated the French language and culture made them the most appropriate of all our protégés to take charge of their own destiny.

I believe, therefore, that sooner or later France could have opened proceedings that would have given the Vietnamese their independence—or at least a progressive autonomy—and that France could have maintained useful relations with the Vietnamese people, to whom she was attached and who were attached to her.

World War II had left France weakened, impatient, confused, and unable to deal with a jumbled mass of problems. Brutally cornered, the French were obliged to carry out hastily an operation that could be successfully carried out only calmly and coolheadedly. The half-measures that could have "saved face" and protected our national interests were no longer practicable. We had to risk everything.

The action of Admiral Thierry d'Argenlieu has often been condemned. In his defense I will say that in 1945 it was impossible for a man of his rank to imagine that to make concessions in Indochina was not equivalent to a capitulation that would risk handing over the country to the Communists. That was the way he viewed the problem.

As for me, I believe that Ho Chi Minh was as much a Nationalist as a Communist and that we should have taken that risk. The political régime in North Vietnam would perhaps be less harsh than it is today had we, at the beginning of the war, yielded on the essentials. Rather than attempting, as we did, to remove Cochin China from the Democratic Republic of Vietnam by a kind of *diktat,* we should have allowed the population to decide their destiny by the referendum that had been agreed upon. The results would no doubt have been different then from what they would be today or in any case would have been carried out under more satisfactory conditions.

"Yes, but your solution would not have lasted ten years," is what I have often been told. And the skeptics continue by saying, "The Vietnam 'hawks' would gradually have nibbled away the few positions we had conserved and would have tried to win over the entire country to communism."

Yes, I admit that is possible, but what then? Have we not arrived at a result much worse with the war? We would at least have been spared a war, we would not have shamed and demoralized our army, and we would have conserved an intellectual and moral influence if not an economic advantage. I can say this with certitude since, as we shall see, even after that atrocious war the bonds that had been formed with

Vietnam during the eighty years of cohabitation were not broken.

Besides, the example of India is there to strengthen my point of view. When I was told what Admiral Lord Mountbatten said in 1948 when he relinquished British power in India and handed the country over to native rule, I felt more melancholy than vain. "I am doing in India," he said, "only what Jean Sainteny wanted to do in Indochina."

The war increased all the problems, and invariably it ultimately served the very communism it had hoped to nip in the bud by taking up arms against it. We understand this better today.

But the saddest thing is that our Indochinese experience in the years 1945–1954 has not served as a lesson either to us or to our allies, for it was from the Franco-Vietnamese conflict that sprang the American-Vietnamese war, which, at this writing, has been threatening world peace for seven years.*

---

* The duration is seven years if we count from the Tonkin Gulf "incident" and the sending to Vietnam of an American force of over twenty thousand soldiers, but it is fourteen years if we count from 1957, when the first American casualties were announced. However, the American wounded and dead were termed "advisers" to the South Vietnamese armies.—*Translator's note.*

9

EIGHT YEARS LATER

July 21, 1954. Night was falling on the Mediterranean as our little sloop left the San Remo and stood out toward Corsica, all sails spread to catch the faint breeze. In the silence the radio blared the news: an accord had been signed at Geneva between France and Vietnam. The Indochinese war had ended.

I was aroused from deep thought by the shout of my companion.

"Looks as though our cruise is over before it gets started? Right?"

All night long I remained at the tiller, my thoughts in far-off Indochina. Eight years of war had been necessary to bring us back to the point where we began in 1946, before the signing of the preliminary agreements I had concluded with Ho Chi Minh. No, there was a slight difference. France

103

was now in the position of a defeated country, and the hearts and minds of the French were irreparably hurt.

Scarcely had we dropped anchor on July 24 in the port of Ajaccio when my companion's prophecy was fulfilled. The port administrator approached me with the news that Minister of Colonies Guy La Chambre had summoned me to Paris. He wanted to talk matters over.

I returned to Paris that afternoon by the last Air France plane, and next day, July 25, Premier Pierre Mendès-France informed me through Philippe Baudet, his department manager, that he wanted me to represent France in Hanoi. This had been decided during the talks he had had at Geneva with Pham Van Dong after the signing of the agreements.

These 1954 agreements included the following clauses: *

1. The forces of the two parties shall be regrouped on either side of the 17th parallel: those of the People's Army of Vietnam to the north of the line, those of the French Union to the south (this was the essential point).

2. The two zones shall be provisionally administered by the commanders-in-chief of the two parties—one by the Vietminh, the other by the Franco-Vietnamese—until the time of the general elections, which will permit the Vietnamese population to vote on the reunification of the desired régime.

3. These elections shall be held July 20, 1956; they will be prepared from July 20, 1955, onward by consultation between Saigon and Hanoi.

---

* The wording and the numbering of these clauses are the author's. —*Translator's note.*

4. An International Commission for Supervision and Control (I.C.C.) will supervise the withdrawal and regroupment of troops to the north and south of the 17th parallel and will likewise supervise the elections.

5. This commision shall be composed of representatives of Canada (the Western bloc), Poland (the Communist bloc), and India (the "Third World"). The latter, in its quality of a "nonaligned" state, will preside and serve as chairman.

6. The U.S.S.R. and the United Kingdom, who had conjointly presided over the Geneva Conference, will supervise the applications of these agreements, and they will be held accountable by the Control Commission for the execution of its mission.

This mission promised to be a difficult one. The retreat of the armies of the French Union of the north zone posed some especially complex problems. A rigorous agenda had been established, fixing for each region the delays of evacuation, the latest date being May 19, 1955, three hundred days after Geneva. The zone of Haiphong was to be the last zone evacuated.

In fact, despite the apprehensions over the ten-month period of cohabitation provided for by a very daring clause in the agreements, the respective withdrawals of troops were effected according to plan and without notable incidents. The credit for this success should be given to both commands. It gave hope that the resumption of contacts between the formerly belligerent nations would be less difficult than had been feared.

On the other hand, one had every reason to wonder what the feelings of the Vietnamese people would be regarding the partition of their country, even a temporary partition as was provided for by Article 1 in the Geneva agreements. It was a "fashionable" solution, having been applied in Korea to prevent the fire from spreading. Unfortunately it recalled another partition of former times, symbolized by the ancient wall of Dong Hoi that had been raised by the Trinh, the lords of the North, and the Nguyen, the lords of the South, during their fratricidal war.

In the negotiations south of the 17th parallel France was represented by General Ely, Delegate-General of France, a strong and respected personality who became, in the natural course of events and by gradual changes, a veritable ambassador. He was even more than that, since he eventually held the title of Commander-in-Chief of the French troops that would still remain in the five territories of the old Indochinese Union.

North of the 17th parallel the goals assigned to the representative of France, whose title remained to be defined, were to be essentially the following:

1. To try to resume contact with our recent enemies and former protégés;
2. To avoid such incidents as are always to be feared on such occasions during the time of the French withdrawal of troops;
3. To facilitate the departure of French colonials desirous of leaving Tonkin;
4. To supervise the maintenance of those who desire to remain there;
5. To present to both parties the matters in dispute, such as the costs, which threaten to be considerable;
6. To provide for the continuation of our cultural institutes in North Vietnam.

When these aims were put before me by Pierre Mendès-France, I refused his offer to appoint me the French representative for North Vietnam, and I immediately returned to Corsica.

I refused because I disliked the idea of having to play the part of a liquidator and felt I could no longer be of use to Hanoi after a war that had doubtless destroyed what remained of Franco-Vietnamese friendship. Besides, the proceedings used against me in 1947 upon my return to France, with a view of discrediting, in my person, the policy of conciliation to which my name was attached, had led me to remain aloof from Indochinese affairs. I had even refused, at the time of the Geneva Conference, Georges Bidault's invitation to assist him in those negotiations.

But when I returned from Corsica to Paris early in August, Pierre Mendès-France gave me to understand that he still depended on me. I talked it over with some of Mendès-France's colleagues and other people who could clarify the meaning and amplitude of the proposed mission, and on August 11 I paid a visit to the Rue de Solferino, where General de Gaulle received visitors every Wednesday. When I told him of my hesitation, I drew from him this retort: "Well, can you think of anyone else to send to Hanoi?" This sally inclined me to accept the proposed task.

On August 15 Pierre Mendès-France, whom I barely knew but with whom I had had a long conversation on Asian problems, invited me to his home in Marly. We had a long talk about the aspects of the problem and the possible developments of the mission he wanted to entrust to me. He agreed absolutely with me in my desire to act as "a continuer and not a liquidator" during my mission in Hanoi. He said he had been impressed at Geneva by the remarks of the Vietnamese delegation. Several times they had declared their desire to conserve in Vietnam a French presence, for they still recognized such a need.

Mendès-France was greatly attracted to the possibility of France's return to Tonkin, thus penetrating Communist Asia, particularly on the very frontiers of worrisome China, which had become Mao's China and remained totally withdrawn from the rest of the world.

"When you are there in Hanoi, you will be occupying a balcony overlooking China," he told me.

That is the way I interpreted my position, and this aspect of my mission made it all the more interesting. After all, the main talk of the time was of "peaceful coexistence," and our future relations with the Democratic Republic of Vietnam could amount to an experiment that might teach us many valuable lessons.

But difficulties lay ahead, and when I left the oasis of peace in Marly that sunny August 15, I foresaw the storms that loomed on the horizon at the other end of the world. Could I manage, as they expected of me, to save what could still be saved? Would I be able to renew friendly relations with the men who only yesterday were France's most bitter enemies and resume with Ho Chi Minh the dialogue that had been interrupted December 3, 1946? How much simpler it would have been to remain in Tonkin, even at the cost of relinquishing our sovereignty! How much more difficult it was to return after eight years of war!

I arrived in Saigon on August 27, and there, before going to Hanoi, I conferred with General Ely, who proved to be rather skeptical about the results of my mission and was obviously worried about the difficulties it could cause him in South Vietnam.

After the talk with General Ely I had an interview with the President of South Vietnam, Ngo Dinh Diem, whom I knew quite well and with whom I was on good terms—although he was far from being a Francophile. He received me cordially, but he did not conceal his disappointment at seeing me represent France in North Vietnam, where I would deal with his fraternal enemies, the Communists. This reaction, by the way, forecast the difficulties I would eventually encounter. To his mind, my mission was the equivalent of France's *de facto* recognition of the Hanoi government. Thus our relations were to become progressively more strained until I was ultimately interdicted from the territory of South Vietnam.

I arrived in Hanoi August 31 and was welcomed only by the French notables who happened still to be in North Vietnam. Ho Chi Minh's government had not yet been established in the capital.

It is needless to list here all the questions I had to cope with immediately. It is enough to say that I spent September 5 and 6 talking with the principal surviving defenders of Dienbienphu, who had been liberated only a few days before. Most of them were still undergoing treatment in the Lannessan hospital. Among others I talked to were the officers Castries, Lalande, Langlais, Bigeard, and Blanchet.

In the remarks of these heroes it was easy to note a real esteem for the fighting qualities of their adversaries—qualities that the French government and many French military chiefs had unfortunately underestimated. Their evaluation of the enemy accentuated the bitterness they felt about the futility of the sacrifices to which they had been obliged to consent during the almost eight years of war. They gave me messages for their families, which I transmitted, with emotion, upon my return to Paris a few days later.

I had asked Premier Mendès-France to let me study the situation on the spot before giving him my definitive acceptance of the post. Summing up my impressions of the situation, I found them sufficiently encouraging to impel me to plunge into the task that many considered hopeless, and on October 6 I left for Hanoi duly endowed with the title (chosen by the premier) of General Delegate of the French Republic to the Democratic Republic of Vietnam. *

As I crossed the Doumer bridge upon my arrival in Hanoi, I met Colonel Lefebre d'Argencé, who was leaving the town with the last French detachment. Many newspapers published the picture of us as we stood there together. The photographs taken do not show one important thing: the tears that ran down the face of the old soldier during his impeccable salute before our final embrace. It took a great deal of faith in the future to forget that moving sight.

A meeting with Ho Chi Minh had not been scheduled for me during my previous short visit to Hanoi. Indeed, Paris had recommended that I avoid "all personal and direct contact" with him until the situation had cleared a little.

Besides, the President of the Democratic Republic of Vietnam had not yet reinstalled himself in Hanoi and did not do so until September 10, when elements of the people's army of Vietnam very quietly entered the capital. This detachment included the famous Division 308, which had conquered the French at Dienbienphu.

A few days after my arrival the second time Vice-Premier and Minister of Foreign Affairs Pham Van Dong sent word that he would receive me on September 17 at the "palace."

Little had changed in the pseudolavish furnishings of that palace so ill-suited to the tropics since our superior residents

---

* This title, *Délégué général du Gouvernement de la République française auprès de la République démocratique du Vietnam*, is preserved by my successors to the post.

in Tonkin had formerly occupied it. It was now apparently the seat of government chosen by the executive branch of the Democratic Republic of Vietnam, and Ho Chi Minh would soon be giving his official audiences and receptions there.

Pham Van Dong had likewise not changed in the least. Tall (for a Vietnamese), slender, calm, he had always been hollow-cheeked, with the same attentive and burning gaze. His dark gray uniform, buttoned formally to the neck, gave him a certain Spartan elegance. The guerrilla warrior had become a true statesman. Although he had not entirely rid his speech of a slight foreign accent, his French was of a rare quality; one recognized in his language the professor he had once been.

We exchanged memories and discussed general subjects. Then to my surprise, the door opened, and Ho Chi Minh came in. His entrance was as quiet as it was unexpected.

Was this man really Ho Chi Minh?

Various rumors, some of which seemed credible, had reached my ears, as they had reached those of others, that the President of the Democratic Republic of Vietnam had died during the war in the course of a bombardment. The rumors stated that a "double" for Ho had been substituted for public appearances so that the people should always remain unaware that their idol was no longer alive to guide them.

Pham Van Dong, aware perhaps of the surprise that had been planned for me, had stood up and was smiling as I gazed at the unexpected apparition.

A single glance was enough to cancel as sheer stupidity the tags of gossip about the death of Ho Chi Minh. This was indeed Ho Chi Minh standing before me, and that day as formerly he was at the head of the Democratic Republic of Vietnam. The eight hard years that had passed since 1946 had no doubt left their mark. His shoulders sagged, his goatee and hair had whitened, and by contrast his skin seemed yellower, with the gleam of old ivory. Although his body had kept its youthful slenderness, his face had filled out a little and become almost chubby, thus giving him the benevolent aspect suitable to the personality of the "good uncle" to whom his people often referred. The things that had not changed about him were the fervor and mobility of his eyes and the inimitable mixture of reserve and vivacity in his bearing.

Thus we were face to face for the first time since our meeting on December 3, 1946, when, as anxious and ill as he then had been, he had not concealed from me his apprehensions about the future.

Ho Chi Minh must have been as embarrassed as I. Like mine, his mind's eye must have seen the images of the implacable struggle that had drawn the Vietnamese people into a ferocious war against our expeditionary forces. Only a few hundred yards away from this tranquil reception room was the pavement of the Avenue Borgnis-Desbordes, where I had been left for dead on December 19, 1946, when the mine set by the friends of Ho Chi Minh had exploded.

It was not unlikely that he was thinking of this at that very moment, yet his hesitation did not last more than a few instants. Then he held out his arms to me.

"Well, shall we not embrace?" he asked.

And we gave each other the ceremonial hug and kiss.

"You see?" he continued. "We have fought, we have struck out at each other for eight years, but honorably. Now that is done with. You must stay here, and with the same fairness we will come to an agreement and will work together like partners, going—how do you say it?—fifty-fifty."

"We will work together." No doubt he wanted this but only under certain conditions, the first of which was diplo-

matic reciprocity. If a satisfactory solution were not found
to this very delicate question, it could compromise to the
point of rendering untenable our attempt at coexistence.

As Delegate General of the French Republic I did not
have, properly speaking, diplomatic status; this would only
be recognized when France admitted the presence in Paris
of a General Delegate of the Democratic Republic of
Vietnam, my counterpart.

Already the drafting of my credentials had been so labori-
ous that I was unable to present that document to Ho Chi
Minh until December. It was a cautious text, which ap-
preciably restricted the scope of my mission and was bound
to disappoint the Vietnamese government.

But Ho Chi Minh pretended to consider me as a fully
qualified ambassador. He even recognized me tacitly at once
as doyen of the diplomatic corps—a status that was justifi-
able in view of the many years I had spent in Tonkin, the importance of the mission I headed, and the French interests
that still existed in Vietnam. But it was essentially a gesture
of courtesy and good will, perhaps also of personal esteem.

In the course of an afternoon tea given on December 20
by Pham Van Dong in my honor and in honor of the French
notables present in Hanoi, Ho Chi Minh again showed his
good will by joining us "unexpectedly" for a few minutes and
asking me to introduce those of my compatriots who were
present.

Little by little I lost this favorable treatment when the
Hanoi government became aware that France did not intend
to accord diplomatic reciprocity. It was the beginning of a
long and regrettable misunderstanding, the installation in
Paris in 1956 of a North Vietnamese commercial attaché
serving as a makeshift. Indeed, as is well known, it was not
until the return to power of General de Gaulle in 1966 that

the French government finally invited the Democratic Republic of Vietnam to send a Delegate General to Paris.*
(Ironically enough, when the general returned to power in 1958, the authorities of the Democratic Republic of Vietnam fell into step with the French Communist party by organizing demonstrations against "the Gaullist Fascists.")

What in the world were the reasons that prevented Premier Mendès-France and those who succeeded him from making that gesture of reciprocity so much desired by Hanoi? Indubitably the reserves expressed by South Vietnam and the Americans, who, realizing their error in having supported the Vietminh and its leader in 1945 (although they knew Ho Chi Minh's past and his aspirations), now wanted to counterbalance his influence by making South Vietnam a bastion of anticommunism—not only in Indochina but in all Southeast Asia. It was a policy instigated by John Foster Dulles, and it produced the defense pact of Southeast Asia (SEATO) signed at Manila on September 8, 1954.*

Probably alerted by Ngo Dinh Diem, Washington became so alarmed at my presence in North Vietnam that the Quai d'Orsay felt obliged to address a placating telegram minimizing the importance of my mission to such an extent that it was deprived of any substance. As early as September 16, Jean Daridan, Adjutant High-Commissioner in Saigon, had written a personal letter to me saying that the South Viet-

---

* The person appointed was Mai Van Bo, chief of the Commercial Delegation of the D.R.V. He was given the title of Delegate General on May 23, 1967, and at this writing he is still at this post in the French capital, where his qualities have won him much esteem and friendship.

* Moreover, John Foster Dulles kept me waiting to present my credentials by rejecting all the formulas of wording prepared by France (we actually submitted them to him for his approval), and I had had to fight to obtain a text that was not totally devoid of significance.

namese government (which had adhered to the SEATO pact
during the interval) apparently regretted the step taken
toward Hanoi and that I should wait for the return of General Ely from Washington; the general had gone there with
the French Minister of Foreign Affairs to obtain some indication of what actions I would be free to take in the Democratic Republic of Vietnam.

At that time we had neither the material nor the morale
to risk aggravating the United States. Nor did we want to
imperil the important interests we still had in South Vietnam
—interests we felt had more chance of being preserved than
by according the Communist government at Hanoi equal
recognition.

This is all quite understandable. What is less so is the lack
of a concerted policy. After all, any action I could take in
North Vietnam was no less useful than what our embassy
could take in South Vietnam—for all the reasons I have
given. Why, then, should we not be represented in the two
zones of our former Indochina? Besides, it is not at all certain
that South Vietnam would have been more accommodating
had we yielded to its desires and suppressed our representation in Hanoi. On the contrary, the leaders of South Vietnam
could have interpreted such a gesture as a sign of weakness
and might have become more exigent and hostile.

Finally, if the Vietminh had triumphed in the elections
provided for in the Geneva agreements and thus become the
masters of a unified Vietnam (as many observers predicted),
would this not have made it a serious error on the part of
France not to have maintained diplomatic contact from the
beginning?

Guy La Chambre is reported to have made this comment:
"With Ely in Saigon and Sainteny in Hanoi I'm prepared for
anything." This teamwork was never put into effect, and in

fact the idea was soon abandoned. General Ely considered the two missions rivals; I considered them complementary.

Our Hanoi delegation was more and more subjected to a suspicious attitude on the part of our Saigon embassy. Perhaps the diplomatic personnel that we maintained in Saigon felt that a part of the French government and public opinion disapproved of our representing France at Hanoi; perhaps, too, by a weird kind of mimetism that occurs not infrequently, our embassy had become infected by the surrounding political atmosphere and was adopting the age-old animosity that had made the South oppose the North in Vietnam, cruelly revived by the partitioning of the country imposed by the Geneva agreements. Again, an old phenomenon was blurring the view of the Indochinese problem: in Saigon they were unable to see the forest for the trees.

I regretted all the more this lack of cooperation since I had in front of my eyes the admirable example of the British, whose consulate in Hanoi was given complete support by their embassy in Saigon.

Her Majesty's government had not yet officially recognized North Vietnam, but with the traditional policy of the British it had "forgotten" that it had a consulate in Hanoi, which it had maintained before the Geneva treaty. It had been called a "consulate general's" post, but it was nonetheless very modest, since it was composed of only three diplomats under the direction of Geoffrey Baker. The daily lives of the diplomats were brightened only by games on the tennis court of our delegation* and by dinner parties at the homes of non-Communist diplomats—that is to say, the Canadian and Indian

---

* At the beginning of my mission some Vietnamese functionaries either authorized themselves or were authorized to play on that tennis court. This privilege was brief.

representatives on the International Commission of Control. Otherwise the Consulate General of Great Britain had no official existence at all.

Even so, those three British members of the "forgotten" consulate did meet Pham Van Dong one day. It was at a reception we gave in celebration of July 14, 1956, and I introduced the consul.

"May I present the Consul of Great Britain . . . ."

The more phlegmatic Englishman of the two was not the one you would suppose but Pham Van Dong.

"Ah, yes?" he said, with admirable calm mixed with polite interest. "I did not know there was a British consulate in Hanoi."

The Englishman took it with a smile, and his restraint was later rewarded. A few weeks later he was being invited to all the official receptions of the Democratic Republic of Vietnam, though he was accorded a place far below the salt.

So as not to be obliged to expel the American representatives, the North Vietnamese authorities managed gradually to "asphyxiate" them, and it almost solely was because of the General Delegation of France that the American consulate was able to stay on to the end of 1954 in spite of everything that transpired. That consulate's last manifestation was at a reception it gave for Thanksgiving Day. Aside from the British and the French, only the Canadians and Indians of the International Control Commission came—very timidly. The only Vietnamese present were the *can-bo* (political delegates), who stood outside the entrance, carefully jotting down the license numbers of the cars that had brought those guests who had dared to accept the Americans' invitation! It was rather delightfully paradoxical, in a country that was rich in paradoxes at that time, to see the American consulate aided in its ephemeral existence by a French delegation that had become the *bête noire* of the state department. Indeed, we were regarded as such a nuisance that the United States redoubled pressures against the French government to force it to renounce any French representation in North Vietnam. We had certainly been through worse.

The Communist countries were, of course, represented in Hanoi, but diplomatic life gravitated to the embassies of mainland China and Soviet Russia, both very important and active and apparently on the best of terms with each other.

Yet from this time forward it was easy to note the symptoms of Sino-Soviet rivalry. This contest between the two Communist powers to attain an ascendency over the Democratic Republic of Vietnam was perhaps the first indication of a rivalry that has today become a veritable hostility.

Already in 1954 the U.S.S.R. established in Hanoi a formidable diplomatic representation, headed by "strong man" Ambassador Lavritchev, who had distinguished himself in Bulgaria in 1944 when Soviet troops occupied Sofia. Lavritchev manifested the intention of exercising a widespread influence over this new people's republic in Asia.

At first the North Vietnamese regarded Soviet Russia as the ranking leader of the Eastern countries, an admired, respected, and constantly consulted "big sister." However, it soon became evident that the Soviets disliked their mission and the country in which it was established. Whether out of lassitude or because of an entente between Moscow and Peking, it was noted toward the year 1956 that the Russians were delegating leadership to the Chinese.

How did Ho Chi Minh exercise his influence in this rivalry of the two Communist powers? Commentators on this time have all too readily termed him the leader of the Moscow faction. His past, his frequent visits to Moscow, and the part he had played with Borodin seemed to prove this, whereas his misunderstandings with China and the fact that he had spent some time in Chinese prisons and had fought Chinese intervention in his own country seemed to indicate that he could not possibly be pro-Chinese in this turn of events. In addition, the generation to which he belonged had not forgotten that the Chinese were the traditional enemy-invader; this, added to the recent and poignant memory of the way the Yunnan army had come in 1945 to disarm the Japanese troops in accordance with the provisions of the Potsdam treaty and had then put down roots in the territory north of the 16th parallel, seemed to indicate that he would prefer the Russian teachers who had formed his youthful mind rather than the descendants of those who had been the oppressors of his ancestors.

I recall that the behavior of the Chinese troops and their commanders in 1945 had left no doubt of their final objective: it was in great part to get rid of that menacing presence that the old revolutionary, now President of the Democratic Republic of Vietnam, sought an entente with France. I recall Ho Chi Minh's wry comment: "Far better to smell the dung of the French than to eat Chinese dung all one's life!"

But Ho Chi Minh was an Asian. His culture was profoundly Chinese. He rivaled the most distinguished Chinese scholars in his mastery of their language, being able to express himself with equal ease in Cantonese or Mandarin. He could even—as some of his ministers have told me—use the language as a kind of shorthand, taking notes in Chinese characters during meetings and conferences.

Above all, from 1945 Ho knew that his friend and counterpart Mao Tse-tung, whose destiny ran parallel to his own, would sooner or later be the master of China, the largest and most densely populated country in the world and the most powerful neighbor of little Vietnam.

China was powerful, but she had been converted to new ideas. Because they were waging the same combat against Western tutelage and were inspired by the same xenophobic nationalism, Democratic Vietnam and the People's Republic of China, welded together as they were by Marxist-Leninist thought, would not and could not confront each other as enemies. Instead they must communicate in a fraternal and productive understanding.

The last thoughts Ho Chi Minh may have allowed himself on this subject before his death were not devoid of some bitterness. China of the imperial dynasties, China of the Kuomintang, China of the people—eternal China would never renounce Tonkin, that "little nation that serves only to protect the frontier provinces of Yunnan and Kuang-si," which "we can never abandon." These words appear in a Chinese document of 1882.

One is therefore tempted to believe that, faithful in this instance to his methods, Ho Chi Minh tried to maintain a delicate balance between China and Russia, as he did between his pro-Chinese and pro-Soviet collaborators. If we may allow that he succeeded in this action until his death, what about his successors? Will they be as adroit as their old leader? Deprived of the clever mediation of Ho Chi Minh, will they prevent the abyss from deepening between the two great nations, the two social attitudes?

This was perhaps why Ho Chi Minh, in his last will and testament, exhorted China and the U.S.S.R. to put an end to their differences. In that testament we find these words:

Having dedicated my whole life to the cause of the revolution, I am all the more proud to see the international Communist and workers' movement expand, and I suffer all the more because of the dissension that at present divides the Communist powers. I want our party to do its best to contribute efficaciously to the reestablishment of good relations between the Communist powers. . . . I firmly believe that the fraternal parties and countries will one day be reunited. . . .

The world has seen in these words a supreme recommendation urging the Chinese and the Soviets to silence their grievances and to resume their interrupted dialogue. We remember that Kosygin, who represented the U.S.S.R. at Ho Chi Minh's funeral, kept the plane that took him from Moscow to Hanoi so that he could make a detour to Peking to talk with Chou En-lai. Yet Kosygin seemed not to have noticed the presence of Chinese Vice-Premier Li Hsien-hien, seated a few yards away from him on the official platform at that funeral.

Did the Russians and the Chinese try to respect the dying wishes of their old Vietnamese comrade? It is hard to say. More probably the two great Communist powers had come to realize that their growing antagonism, although for internal reasons it might serve a purpose, risked plunging them into an ideological abyss, and both powers sought a way of renewing their compromised relations without "losing face." In accepting the posthumous mediation of Ho Chi Minh, they found the pretext they had been seeking. Thus they rendered homage to the man who had made the appeal without having to fear that the authority they recognized might arouse anxiety and make of the dead man a third "great power."

10

HO CHI MINH AND HIS FOLLOWERS

THE atmosphere in Hanoi at the beginning of the Communist régime was quite strange.

The political commissars, called *can-bo,* were suspicious and meddlesome busybodies, organizing meetings, patriotic chorals, processions, indoctrination sessions, early morning calisthenics, and so on. This activity was intended to condition a naturally skeptical and irreverent population.

For the hundred French citizens who had followed me to Hanoi (predominantly professors and functionaries of the delegation), the police surveillance was very strict. There was no question of traveling around the city without a pass, not even to take a stroll or to go to the airport. Two armed soldiers kept perpetual guard at our door and at the doors of all official buildings used by us, and they diverted pedestrians to the opposite side of the street.

123

But there were holes in this net, and one felt that the men in charge were uncertain of how to proceed. By and large the conditions were more like those of China in the "Hundred Flowers" period than those in Stalinist Russia.

For example, only the *can-bo* wore the soldiers' and workers' blue outfit. Some of the merchant class remained faithful to the European clothing worn in colonial times; the artisans, peasants, and the humble people kept to their traditional brown *cunao,* and some of the young women still made the streets colorful with their long slit tunics worn over black silk pants and their big conical hats of straw tied at the neck with bright-colored ribbons.

Just as the population was motley in its attire, it was frequently heterodox in its remarks, at least those addressed to us. Some curio merchants whom I had known for a long time took me into the back rooms of their shops to show me antique pottery, explaining that the objects displayed in the show windows were good enough for the Russians, "who don't know anything about antique pottery." Similarly, a number of artists living and working together, occupied in producing "Socialist realism" art, though they did not complain, hung on the wall of their workshop a big photograph of a sculpture by Rodin. And I can never forget the old Buddhist priestess who stood silent under the propaganda posters that had been pasted up in her pagoda beside a portrait of Ho Chi Minh, explaining to me that she did not know what the posters meant, for she could only read Sanskrit!

In short, many Vietnamese did not hesitate to say they hated to adopt the usages of the new China, even the blue jumpsuits and beaked cap à la Mao; whether Communist or not, they said, "The Chinese are always Chinese."

Many even in official circles were not averse to critical discussion. One evening when we were dining in a government villa, the wife of a minister put a direct question to my wife. "Tell me, Madame," she said, "what do you think about the new Vietnam, the new régime?"

My wife replied that she had the greatest sympathy for the Vietnamese, that she appreciated the efforts being made by the government in many domains, but that she found it difficult to approve, in a general way, communism as practiced since Lenin's death. She quoted Camus on the subject: "I cannot approve a régime that condemns to prison or death fifty million men. . . ."

"Oh, come, how do you arrive at that number?" asked someone at the table.

"But to what is your Camus alluding?" asked another.

And so it went until finally the lady who had put the original question cut short the dialogue, no doubt sensing its incongruity and perils.

"Anyway," she said curtly, "the number of victims doesn't matter; all that matters is the result."

The remarks made to us were rarely that cynical, but they were often of such frankness that one could hardly fail to believe their sincerity.

One evening as I was dining with the Minister of Public Health, a man who had resided for many years in France, the conversation turned to the subject of dogs, which, in imitation of China, the Democratic Republic of Vietnam was planning to eliminate. The wife of one of my colleagues, who had just arrived from Paris, was astounded, and she took up the defense of the threatened canines.

"But, sir," the woman said, "dogs are very useful animals at times for old people or as watchdogs against thieves. . . ."

The minister turned to her and said, gently but firmly, as if giving a lesson to a child: "Madame, you forget: there are no more thieves in Vietnam."

This statement was all the more piquant since several typewriters had been stolen from the premises of our General Delegation only the night before.

Ho Chi Minh was above such talk. He never replied to questions with the total lack of humor shown by some of his ministers, although such lack of humor is the common characteristic of Communist leaders, a surprising trait since the Vietnamese people had in the past always demonstrated a critical and mocking spirit.

Indeed, when I conversed with Ho Chi Minh, I was amazed at how rarely he referred to the ideas and the men who had directed or, more correctly, determined his destiny and his actions. No doubt he realized that propaganda would have been wasted on me, and he did not want to expose himself to ridicule by trying it. In contrast to those of his contemporaries whose experiences paralleled his own, he knew how to avoid becoming a slave to the theories he had embraced. Obviously it would be false to say that his methods of thought, his arguments, and his dialectic were unaffected by his philosophical and political commitments, but they were never overburdened with them.

We must not forget that Ho Chi Minh, born in 1890, had not been nurtured from infancy on Socialist theories. Although he later studied them thoroughly, he was, in their regard, self-educated. In his youth he had had a traditional education, limited since his studies were directed by a rather elementary Mandarinate. Added to this education was the general culture he had acquired in his travels, especially during his stays in Paris, and these experiences had sufficed to develop in him that faculty of analysis, that pliability and intellectual curiosity he employed so ably throughout his life. Thus the Marxist theories he espoused had grown in a fertilized terrain, and although he was totally won over to them and had become their apostle, he had not been so overcome as to lose all critical sense. He was, above all, pragmatic, and he was always careful to adopt doctrine to realities. Hence it would seem that very early, if not immediately upon his conversion, this leader of the Vietminh refused to consider Marxism-Leninism as a panacea applicable indiscriminately to all countries. Quite correctly he seems to have deemed Vietnam a particular case, posing specific problems that had to be considered separately.

In fact, the geographical situation of the country, its past history, its customs, its long development under Chinese influence, and the deep imprint left on it by France combined to present a complex of unusual difficulties for the new leaders of the country.

We cannot too often repeat that Ho Chi Minh was firmly convinced that only the teachers he had chosen could permit him to follow the road he had traced for himself and to attain his objectives. But he also realized that he would have to respect certain features of Vietnamese civilization and never to lose sight of them. Again, he was right.

For example, after a badly executed and systematic persecution of the Roman Catholics the government attempted to substitute for the Roman hierarchy a schismatic church, inspired by the experiment in Poland (priests who "loved their country"). Later, when this unfortunate experiment was defeated and as the number of conversions to the Roman Catholic faith constantly increased, Hanoi relaxed its approach to the problem. I can never forget how moved I was at the midnight Christmas Mass, which filled the cathedral with a reverent throng, overflowing onto the *parvis* and counting among its number many uniforms of the people's army of the Democratic Republic of Vietnam.

This liberal position, which may seem surprising on the part of a government of orthodox communism, was probably due, in large part, to the personal influence of its inspirer and chief.

Many other instances of Ho's pragmatism could be cited, but I will mention only a very remarkable one. In the beginning, the élite thinkers in the new government pretended not to understand French; for a short time the leaders considered adopting English as the official language, although almost no one spoke it in North Vietnam. The folly of these ideas was soon noted, and they were abandoned.

I recall a lecture given at the medical school in Hanoi by a visiting French professor, which was interpreted, phrase by phrase, into Vietnamese for the benefit of the students. It very soon appeared that the students were as bored as we were by the interpretation, all the more useless since the technical terms, having no equivalent in Vietnamese, were repeated just as they were by the interpreter.

This sort of thing was soon abandoned, but it was understandable in the beginning; it was meant to encourage national pride in a people who disliked owing anything to their former colonial teachers.

I also remember the parents of school children who complained that their offspring had to learn Russian and Chinese in school, languages that are almost as difficult for the Vietnamese as they are for the French.*

On the personal plane, Ho Chi Minh had not changed at all. His accession to the presidency, the prestige that had accompanied his triumph, the fame he had acquired (mea-

---

* It must be remembered that, thanks to Monsignor de Rhodes, Vietnamese writing had been transliterated and Romanized in the seventeenth century.

sured by the numerous articles appearing about him in the world press), and the many requests for interviews that journalists made had not altered his character. He still retained some of the timidity that had characterized him in his youth. He behaved exactly as he had done with Leclerc, with d'Argenlieu, Georges Bidault, Marius Moutet, and other dignitaries. He remained the same with the celebrities who now paid him visits in Hanoi, celebrities such as Khrushchev, Nehru, Mikoyan, Cyrankievicz, and so on. And it was not the least strange—even touching—trait of his personality.

Was this social awkwardness affected, as some think? No. I believe that his demeanor reflected a certain natural timidity in social contacts, especially with Westerners. I think also that it was an expression of characteristic Oriental courtesy, which dictates humility and self-effacement.

Undeniably, however, there was something of the actor in Ho Chi Minh, and his air of guilelessness was at times irritating.

During his official stay in France, at the conclusion of a banquet at the Hôtel de Ville in Paris he took an orange from the bowl of fruit on the table and gave it to the first little girl he saw in the crowd as he went down the big flight of steps. This was obviously a premeditated gesture for the benefit of the Parisian crowd. But in 1955, at the end of an intimate dinner in the Hanoi Palace, where there were only three guests at his table, when he took the tangerines remaining in the fruit bowl and offered them to my wife, was he playing to the crowd? What motive was he then obeying? Certainly he was not trying to make an impression on me; I knew him too well. His action could only be a reflex inherited from the most ancient traditions of the Vietnamese people, for whom every occasion is a pretext for presenting a gift, no matter how small. This interpretation is, I think, all the more accurate since my wife had just arrived from Paris and the Vietnamese rules of etiquette dictated a welcoming gesture.

Sometimes, no doubt, Ho exaggerated his air of simplicity; that was an aspect of the comedian in him. For instance, there was that official reception in the great hall of the palace in honor of Anastase Mikoyan. Noting that two chairs were missing, Ho said to Mikoyan in French, *"Eh bien, asseyons-nous par terre, à la bonne franquette"*; and giving the example, he sat down on the floor. The joke, followed by the gesture, was perhaps ostentatious. But how many times in his vagabond life had he not been obliged to sit or sleep on the floor? Is it not a habit of the Vietnamese people, especially country folk, to sit on their haunches?

One might say also that the gesture of the old revolutionary was for the benefit of some of the many officers present; among those at the reception there were quite a few with rather rustic manners, and at the buffet there were some who ate chicken with their fingers.

Assuredly Ho Chi Minh was much too shrewd not to realize that his simplicity and his attachment to local customs contributed greatly to his popularity. But his enemies themselves never doubted the genuineness of his manners. How could he have held the pose for such a long time and so perfectly it it were not authentic?

We should remind ourselves that he and all the ministers of his government lived very simply. Although they entertained in the former French palaces, they lived very modestly in cramped quarters or in small villas. Their vow of poverty was never violated.

It is perhaps wise to linger for a moment on the subject of Ho Chi Minh's attitude toward Roman Catholics and toward religion in general; no other trait reveals his character and his political opportunism more clearly.

In proclaiming his attachment to religious freedom, no doubt Ho wanted to prove his liberalism. But one must not underestimate the fact that Tonkin and North Annam, evangelized since the sixteenth century, counted among the population more than one million fervent Roman Catholics. * In 1954 about a half million of those Catholics, fearing repressive laws, fled from North Vietnam and took refuge in the South, answering the summons of Ngo Dinh Diem, who had energetically encouraged the exodus.

However, five or six hundred thousand Catholics chose to remain in the North and held out with admirable consistency against the pressures and occasional persecutions leveled against them. By reaction, there was an increased number of conversions, and the seminary of Tong acquired at this period an unaccustomed number of novices.

Surprised at this state of things and not caring to create martyrs, Ho Chi Minh realized that he would have to reckon with those who, while accepting the laws of the Vietminh, had not given up their religion. While discussing the problem with me, Pham Van Dong divulged the fact that he was very annoyed about the Roman Catholic exodus to the South, and he declared that in a reunited Vietnam there would be no religious persecution.

---

* The second estimate, made in 1950, showed the following approximate numbers for the towns north of the 17th parallel:

Bui Chu	185,000
Phat Diem	100,000
Haiphong	130,000
Bac-Ninh	60,000
Hanoi	200,000
Lang-Son	5,000
Thai-Ninh	120,000
Vinh	170,000
Than Hoa	60,000
Total:	1,030,000

I may say that I personally never detected in any remarks made by Ho Chi Minh the least trace of aggressiveness, skepticism, or irony in regard to any religion whatsoever. I cannot forget that, during his enforced wait in Biarritz, he asked me one day to organize a visit to Lourdes! Always curious to learn, always courteous, he had sincerely wanted to visit the shrine, and in his conversation with Monsignor Théas, who had welcomed him there, he manifested a respectful interest.

In this connection, I am once more reminded of the letter dated February 24, 1947, addressed to me, in which he expressed the hope that God would accord success to our peacemaking efforts, and he called upon Him to bear witness that neither of us was responsible for the war that had ravaged the country since December 19, 1946. Was this merely pretense? If so, whom was he trying to deceive? Certainly not me, and he would be quite certain that I would not make his letter public.*

Moreover, there is that mysterious sentence in his last will and testament, a surprising statement on the part of an atheist: ". . . I am writing these few lines in expectation of the day when I shall go to rejoin the venerable Karl Marx, Lenin, and our revolutionary elders. . . ."

It would be interesting to know *where* this materialist thought of meeting again, after death, the thinkers who had so influenced him, but perhaps in the Far East the idea of atheism does not connote what it does in Europe. There exists in Orientals a kind of diffuse religiosity, which renders less surprising Ho Chi Minh's references to God.

---

* I published his letter only in 1967, in the second edition of my *Histoire d'une paix manqueé.*

Be that as it may, we know that in 1954 and even in 1955 and the following years, the Democratic Republic of Vietnam proclaimed on the occasion of All Saints' Day and Christmas the government's attachment to the principles of freedom of worship. December 24, 1955, was declared a Catholic holiday, and political meetings were suspended so that devout Catholics could attend Mass, as they did in a fervent multitude.

In a message to Vietnamese Roman Catholics, Ho Chi Minh demonstrates his religious tolerance:

. . . on this second Christmas of peace, the populations of the North can freely worship God, the enemy having vacated their churches and no longer persecuting the inhabitants. . . .

Of course, Ho did not lose sight of an opportunity for inserting propaganda, as he does in this document, which continues by recalling that the Catholics "who were forced to evacuate the North and go to the South" must surely be homesick, "fondly remembering their native villages." He concludes by calling upon the "Catholic population to fight for peace and reunification."

Parallel to this effort of Ho Chi Minh at seduction and propaganda, the Committee of Liaison with Patriotic Vietnamese Catholics emphasized reunification, "which is the indisputable desire of the population both of the North and the South." On the other hand, however, the government tried to control religious activities in the country by favoring the creation of a "left-wing clergy," which would establish close relations with left-wing Catholics in central Europe, particularly Poland and Czechoslovakia. Clearly, then, this liberalism was more a surface display than a real one, and it stemmed mainly from political preoccupations.

I must admit that it was very probably due to Ho Chi Minh's influence that I was able to take up the cause of the persecuted French or other Catholic missionaries who were trying to maintain residence in North Vietnam after 1954. In effect, the priests of strict Roman obedience had to give way to the left-wing clergy, and our missionaries, harried time and again by some of the vengeful *can-bo,* denounced by their own parishioners and accused of the most hateful misdeeds, were at best condemned to house arrest or kept strictly under surveillance; sometimes they were chained and incarcerated in makeshift jails.

Very soon I had the impression that this behavior toward Catholic missionaries derived more from local zealots than from any government directive. If I was to be able to put an end to these persecutions, it would be by appealing to the central power, to Pham Van Dong, and to Ho Chi Minh.

The priests and missionaries of Hanoi were not subjected to the same persecutions as those inflicted on their brothers in provincial towns. Monsignor Couhoé, Bishop of Hanoi, after planning to leave the capital, decided to remain when he heard that France was officially returning, and indeed he remained there for many years. On the other hand, Monsignor Mazé, Bishop of Ung Hoa, and Monsignor Hedde, Bishop of Langston, were placed under house arrest, which I myself was able to end.

Upon my insistence, the French priests were freed, and I proceeded to arrange their repatriation. Unfortunately I could do nothing for the native Vietnamese priests.

11

AN ATTEMPT AT
PEACEFUL COEXISTENCE

When the Democratic Republic of Vietnam asked France to be responsible for the maintenance of all French establishments in the territory, it set the hardest test in the attempt at a peaceful coexistence between a capitalist country (France) and a Communist country (North Vietnam).

In 1954 the main public services were still French: railways and street car tracks, water and electricity installations, post offices and telephones, commercial harbors and pilotage, the infrastructure of air travel, and the cultural establishments that were the glory of French colonialism—the Pasteur Institute, the Ecole française d'Extrême-Orient (French School of the Far East), lycées, medical schools, and hospitals. There were some private French enterprises that comprised the essential substructure of North Vietnam: coal

135

mining, breweries and ice-houses, banks, commercial houses, hotels, garages, cemeteries, and workshops of all kinds. Only one important industry, the cotton spinning and weaving firm called the *Cotonnière de Nam-dinh,* escaped the general rule, for its ownership was predominantly Swiss.

In August, 1954, at the talks held between French and Vietnamese experts at Phu-lo, the Vietnamese had clearly expressed the hope, indeed had recognized the need, for our establishments to continue their activities in North Vietnam.

In the course of conversations between Pham Van Dong and me after my return to Hanoi, he kept reverting to this question in more and more urgent terms. Soviet Ambassador Lavritchev came personally to exhort me to act in such a way as to guarantee that the French economic substructure would remain undisturbed. All events lead me to believe that this démarche of the Soviet ambassador was made at the suggestion of his Vietnamese friends.

After prolonged negotiations, a communiqué signed by Phan Anh and Dang Viet Chau, minister and vice-minister of the economy, respectively, reached me on December 10, specifying, at my request, the conditions in which the maintenance of our enterprises would be feasible. The conditions they stated could be considered reassuring, even encouraging, but placed before the perspective of pursuing activities of capitalistic origin in a country of the most orthodox communism, most French enterprises abandoned the attempt. What we knew of the fate reserved to the private Western enterprises that had remained in Shanghai was enough to make us think twice.

As for the Vietnamese, their desire to retain the French enterprises derived mainly from a realistic preoccupation with reestablishing the stability of the country. Added to this was a kind of inferiority complex, which persuaded our former protégés that they would be incapable of taking the place of the French cadres who managed those enterprises—an opinion shared with assurance by those same Frenchmen despite the fact that they had been excellent monitors and were proud of their pupils.

In any event, the opinion held by both factions was wrong. As handy as they are, with a veritable genius for tinkering, after an inevitable period of fumbling and technical accidents the Vietnamese soon made it clear that the French were not indispensable. It is true that they had great help from "friendly countries." Czechoslovakia, Poland, Hungary, and East Germany sent technicians, who spared no pains in their efforts to organize the essential activities that would enable the country to carry on. The Chinese, too, were omnipresent, especially in the vast area of "communications."

Ho Chi Minh entered personally into the important debate and made every effort to retain the French. Did he perhaps lack conviction? Did he not know how to go about it? Or was he merely playing for time, during which the Vietnamese and their "friendly" technicians were able to carry on? Regardless of his motives, Ho's efforts in this direction had little effect.

When I had a meeting with him a few weeks after my return to Hanoi and was beginning to feel that our conversation was leading to nothing positive, I expressed my frustration.

"Well, now," I said, "you wanted me to come here; you wanted France to return. Here I am. What do you expect of me?"

"We have much to do," he replied, "and cannot do everything at once. What we want is for you to take charge of the economic activity of this country. We need your enterprises, and we want them to remain."

I answered that it was above all necessary to inspire the French with confidence.

"We will try to do that," he said.

The Vietnamese government may have thought that these efforts were being made, but to the French the efforts seemed too cautious, insufficient to give them the assurances they needed.

Yet Ho Chi Minh, like Pham Van Dong, continued to press for the French to return and take charge of their establishments. On March 26, 1955, for example, a dinner brought us together for the stated purpose of settling this question once and for all. To begin with, Ho deplored the hostile propaganda raging against my mission. In Saigon, Washington, and even France all possible action was being undertaken to cause my mission to fail. Once more I stressed the absence of guarantees, the lack of any legislation or monetary agreement, and the pestering and chicanery endured by the French enterprises, citing the precedent of Shanghai. All this, I said, legitimately accounted for the skepticism of our French businessmen.

The two Vietnamese statesmen agreed with the points I made, but Ho Chi Minh placed much of the blame on our side.

"All this proves," Ho said, "is that you French are really not fully determined to make an agreement with us. If you were determined, you would be willing to wait until we have time to settle all those difficult problems, for which, we'll admit, we were not prepared. All the same, on the plane of economics and cultural and scientific institutes—in short, everything not connected with the survival of colonialism— you French should desire as much as we do a close collaboration. It is regrettable that you cannot manage to make your compatriots understand this."

I retorted that the best way to help me was to come as quickly as possible to a reasonable settlement of the main issues of our negotiations.

The conversation went on and on without getting anywhere. Ho kept repeating his favorite theme, which he had stated many times during our early negotiations.

"We have fought fairly for eight years," he said. "We can work together fairly now that the war has ended. But this time we will work for the good of our peoples and for our common benefit."

After this dinner I sent a telegram to Paris:

My impression is that the D.R.V. Government is worried about French enterprises forsaking North Vietnam. The leaders see in this abandonment a desire on our part to back the South and leave the North to confront its problems alone with its Socialist allies. They are disappointed at not having inspired confidence, and by their mistrust, procrastinations, indecisions, and imprecisions discouraged French good will and consolidated a negative position held by those who were always hostile to any attempt at coexistence. The D.R.V. will no doubt renew efforts to settle important questions such as the coal mines, for which I believe a solution will be found in the course of next week.* Ho Chi Minh has come to admit that it is easy to give orders but not always easy to have them obeyed. This recognizes the various administrative annoyances about which I complained.

---

* The pact concerning the coal mines was signed April 8, 1955. The French company (La Société française des Charbonnages du Tonkin) was granted an indemnity of five *milliards* [one milliard is equal to one thousand million], representing one million tons of anthracite, to be delivered over a period of fifteen years. The company remained in charge of merchandising.

I believe that the new masters of North Vietnam really wanted to preserve for a time a certain French presence, that they underestimated the legitimate apprehensions felt by merchants, industries, and even by teaching faculties; but they did not know how to impress their wishes upon their agents, who could then have dissipated these fears and conformed to the spirit of the collaboration, the usefulness of which they recognized. And this, I believe, was what Ho Chi Minh implicitly admitted when he said, "It is easy to give orders but not always easy to have them obeyed."

Alas, we know what became of all these good intentions. Although the greater number of French enterprises refused to negotiate and abandoned their installations, depending upon France to obtain indemnities for them later on, a few were able to negotiate and obtain reasonable conditions. However, in these enterprises all or most of their staffs who tried to carry on in North Vietnam were subjected to so much persecution and shabby treatment that they were obliged to pack their bags and leave.

As an example of this sort of thing we can mention the National Enterprise of Coal Mining in Hongay, which had supplanted the Société française des Charbonnages du Tonkin after the accords signed April 8, 1955. At the request of the minister of Vietnamese industry a few French cadres agreed to stay on and collaborate with the North Vietnamese government. It was not their fault that at the end of a short time they gave up, as may be seen by the following report of the outcome that was written and signed by the chief among them:

Note on Religious Freedom under the Régime of the Democratic Republic of Vietnam

The French agents of the S.F.C.T., intending to continue their collaboration at the Coal Mines of Hongay under the D.R.V. régime, had taken care, before the political transfer of the Hongay Zone, April 24, 1955, to ask for formal guarantees from the Minister of Industry and Commerce on the fundamental freedoms they would enjoy (freedom of conscience, notably in political matters; religious freedom; freedom in purchasing food; freedom in housing and travel).

Thus, in the course of the negotiations between the S.F.C.T and the D.R.V., a first delegation led by M. Junqua had drawn up a memorandum entitled "Demand for Guarantees" and had, in the presence of M. Clerget, handed it to M. Phan Anh, Minister of Commerce and Industry, during a particularly cordial audience of February 9, 1955.

M. Phan Anh, having read the document, replied categorically that there could be no problem concerning the respect for and the exercise of individual freedoms under the government of the D.R.V.; that the demands of the French agents were natural and reasonable and that they were consequently granted in advance, with the reservation that some slight alterations be made in the matter of form.

After the signing of the protocol April 8 between the S.F.C.T. and the D.R.V., and before the political transfer of the Hongay Zone that occurred April 24, a new delegation of French agents, led by Messieurs Schulders and Quemener, disposed to collaborate with the new administration of the mines, was received April 14, 1955, by the Deputy-Minister of Commerce and Industry, M. Dang Viet Chau, and solicited a written accord on the guarantees, validating the verbal accord already granted by Minister Phan Anh, as expounded above.

The Deputy-Minister displayed a keen repugnance to the idea of ratifying in writing the promise given by his superior, arguing the futility of inserting in a new text the accord of the D.R.V. government on the demanded guarantees, since the regulations in effect gave the desired assurances.

To the objections of the representatives of the French agents that the aforesaid regulations were unknown to them, our D.R.V. interlocutors replied with a new promise—which was honored to no greater extent than had been the previous one—that these regulations would be assembled under their direction and placed at the disposition of the interested parties.

The representatives of the French personnel kept insisting upon a specific accord on the precise point of religious freedom as set forth in paragraph 2 of their memorandum regarding guarantees of a general order, worded as follows: "The religious freedom of the agents will be full and entire. As a consequence there shall be no impediment to the coming and going of their clergymen in the exercise of their religious duties." M. Dang Viet Chau, in his letter of April 16, 1955, expressed himself as follows: "Religious freedom is placed under the protection of our country's laws to the extent that the religious activities do not violate our laws and regulations and do not derogate the friendly relations between the Vietnamese people and France."

Despite the uneasiness felt by the French delegation over the restrictions inserted in this letter, it relied once more on the verbal promises given by D.R.V. officials and a *laissez-passer* was requested immediately, April 14, by a Dominican priest of Hanoi, the Reverend Père Lena. The document would allow him to be transferred from Hanoi to Hongay, in order to assure the continuation of the parochial ministry there.

For the sake of brevity we omit a description of the multiple police formalities, interrogations, and questionnaires that were inflicted upon the Reverend Père Lena. One anecdote will suffice. He was asked to give the Christian names, employment, addresses, and the family composition of his eleven brothers and sisters!

Despite the efforts of the General Delegation of France in Hanoi and its appeals both to the Ministry of Commerce and to the Ministry of Foreign Affairs, Père Lena was not authorized to go to Hongay before the transfer.

Immediately after the transfer the General Delegation joined its efforts to those of the representatives of the French personnel who had remained in Hongay [. . .], and finally the Ministry of Foreign Affairs agreed to let R. P. Lena have a *laissez-passer*. But the Ministry of Security, under orders from the Workers' party, still objected.

In Hongay Monsignor Clerget, like the representatives of the French personnel, continued to insist on the transfer of the priest, citing the promises of the D.R.V. government. They were always put off. . . .

A typical reply was as follows: "We sincerely want to cooperate with you, but our government is certainly inspired by legitimate motives in taking every precaution in granting the demand of the Reverend Père Lena. We are not acquainted with the particular reasons for the delay in granting the requested *laissez-passer*, but it is natural that our government should become acquainted with the antecedents and mentality of the priest whose transfer to Hongay you desire; in many circumstances French or Vietnamese dignitaries or priests have been persuaded to act, under cover of their priesthood, as reactionary agents of American imperialism." This was signed, Le Viet Huong.

Our refutation to these charges was that the Ministry of Security could at least motivate its refusal; then we would know where we stand, and each of the French agents could come to the decision he judged appropriate on the subject of the continuance of his collaboration. . . .

Weeks and months passed, and the conflict between the security department and the official declarations of the D.R.V. as to religious freedom increased.

In effect, the government was apparently hamstrung by the security department. The National Consultative Assembly of the D.R.V., sitting in Hanoi, voted unanimously a long motion proclaiming religious freedom (visibly destined for propaganda, blaming "the reactionaries" and "the Americans" for the exodus of Vietnamese Catholics to South Vietnam before the transfer of powers). The president of the D.R.V. proclaimed many times on the radio and the press the same doctrine. But the Vice-President, the Minister of Foreign Affairs, and various experts on the economic delegation of the D.R.V. did not conceal the fact that their efforts were not enough to obtain from the security department the *laissez-passer* for the Reverend Père Lena.

On June 14 "The Decree of Religious Freedom" was published, with a long commentary in the July 4 issue of the party's newspaper, *Nhân Dân*. These texts are worth quoting *in extenso*, but we will quote only a few excerpts:

". . . the protection of religious freedom involves the repression of those who create discord in the name of religion." (*Nhân Dân*.)

"When the clergymen of a creed preach religion, they are bound by duty to inculcate their parishioners with a love of the Fatherland, with civic virtues, respect for democratic institutions and for the laws of the D.R.V." (Excerpt from Article 1 of the decree.)

In reality, this decree set forth the principle of the authority of the state over religion.

Moreover, the application of this decree gave rise to various interferences and pressures perpetrated by the state against the religious authorities. We list these as follows:

1. In general, there was constant local propaganda exhorting the faithful not to visit their priests, especially foreign priests. Diocesan presbyteries were under constant surveillance in an effort to identify the "ultras."

2. An ideological dispute began between government representatives, aided by a "Catholic delegation," and the religious authorities, whenever the application of the decree was debated.

These conferences could have pointed out the incompatibility between government pretensions and Catholic obligations, the dogmatic position of Church representatives in Vietnam having been categorically affirmed.

3. On May 23 and the following days there were meetings in Sontay that called together the clergy and some Catholic delegates of the province. The "committal for trial" of Vietnamese and French priests on trifling pretexts was the real aim of the meetings.

4. The *laissez-passer* for the Reverend Père Lena was still not delivered. . . .

It required the intervention of Monsieur Pham Van Dong to extract the authorization for Reverend Père

Lena from the security department. Pham Van Dong was present at the July 14 celebration given by the General Delegation of France, and it was upon the insistence of these French representatives that Pham Van Dong intervened.

Père Lena arrived in Hongay on the afternoon of July 19, but he was obliged to leave on July 25, being summoned to do so by the Hongay *Securitè*. Several pretexts for this summons were given, one being that Hongay was in a "strategic sector."

Other anecdotes no less significant could be added to this report. To mention one out of a hundred examples: it took three weeks for the wife of a French engineer in Hongay to obtain a pass permitting her to go to Hanoi for the purpose of visiting her dentist. She suffered all that time with a toothache.

But there were still more irritating incidents. When a delegation of Frenchwomen (members of the *Union des Femmes*) visited the installations of the coal mines, the Vietnamese guides who showed them around delivered diatribes against the work France had accomplished in Tonkin. (These statements were overheard by one of our engineers.) The guides accused the French government of having left the region of Tonkin in a lamentable state, and they drew a ridiculous and false picture of conditions, going so far as to tell the women—who unfortunately believed them—that there had never been in Hongay a hospital for the native people. In fact, there was indeed a hospital of three hundred and fifty beds, open to all.

It is hard to say to what extent Ho Chi Minh was to blame for the failure of this attempt at cooperation. One thing seems to be clear: his ignorance of economics, which he pretended to discount as of little importance, kept him aloof from this crucial problem. Would the problem have been handled more successfully if he had intervened? Again, it is hard to say. The very idea of attempting cooperation between France and North Vietnam was risky, requiring of both parties an inexhaustible fund of good will and complete forgiveness of the past.

Was Ho Chi Minh acquainted in detail with the conditions of life endured by the French workers, who, attracted to the experiment, tried in spite of the difficulties to carry on their task? Did he know about the impediments put in the path of those French workers by some of his compatriots, who were trying, either consciously or unconsciously, to abort any substantial accomplishment by those Frenchmen? If he was aware of such activities, as he probably was, we must conclude that he was powerless to dampen the zeal of his activists.

No matter what, it is regrettable that at this period, when no one any longer contested the independence of Vietnam, young sowers of discord came between capable leaders and a humble people, so gentle and affable. Those young activists were full of hatred and were obsessed with propaganda, which played a substantial part in sabotaging any beneficial initiative. Naturally, one can choose to believe that their behavior was dictated from above. In that case, however, their immediate chiefs would surely have realized that their actions were much more harmful to Vietnamese interests than to the interests of the French, who, after all, had nothing to lose but their confidence and illusions and who could at any moment return to their native land, where the word "liberty" preserved the meaning it should have, that of permitting one to live and work in peace.

If France failed in her attempt to maintain French institutions in Vietnam—that is to say, our attempt at coexistence—the failure was in great part due to the machinations of those youthful agitators, machinations unworthy of a nation that had come of age.

I cannot believe that Ho Chi Minh approved of this policy of sabotage. The desire he showed for the happiness of his people was too real for him not to have seen the error being made in discouraging those Frenchmen who had agreed to remain in the country. He knew that the maintenance of certain French enterprises, public or private, could have contributed to the well being of the people while procuring for them the employment indispensable to most of them.

France, too, must bear some of the blame for the failure of this experiment, which had seemed so attractive and which, had it been pursued over a longer period of time, would surely have taught us many valuable lessons. The French government should have taken precautions against the risks that would be incurred by the Frenchmen who participated in the experiment. Either the government did not see the necessity, or it simply refused to take any such steps. It soon became clear, when only a bare vestige of French enterprise remained in North Vietnam, that once again a good opportunity had been lost.

(It must be said that some of the French enterprises did not want to be offered the possibility of remaining in Vietnam and rejected the very idea of pacific coexistence. It was more in conformity with their principles or simply more advantageous to claim indemnities from the French government. These indemnities were quite often not obtained, which left the Indochinese colonials worse treated in this respect than the colonials of North Africa.)

In the beginning France had taken the necessary steps for a forthright attempt at coexistence. My mission (as the *Délégation générale de France* was for a long time called) included a number of exceptionally well-qualified men who "played the game" with total integrity, all of them volunteers for a post the drawbacks of which they fully understood. Among them were Admiral Flichy, Hubert Argod, Jean-Baptiste Georges-Picot, Pierre Billecocq, Roland Sadoun, Hubert Dubois, Roger Duzer, Loïc Moreau, Cans, Beauchataud, Professors Bourlière, Huard, Serafino, and many others. I cannot name them all, but all of them tried earnestly and competently to rid their renewed contacts with Vietnam of any rancor or mental reservations.

But in Paris and elsewhere those who took offense at the mission of France in Hanoi contrived to misrepresent its meaning and diminish its scope.

Ho Chi Minh was right when he alluded to "the hostility" that surrounded us. That hostility was in part the hostility of the United States, which was apprehensive about our continuing presence in North Vietnam, believing it would give the Communist party more prestige and authority in Southeast Asia. Some French enterprises in the Haiphong zone (which was the last to be evacuated, three hundred days after the Geneva Convention) even received threats of reprisals if they attempted to continue there.

A Parisian weekly magazine became the self-appointed mouthpiece of this ruinous policy and printed an article attacking our mission in terms as venomous as false, concluding with these words: "One more dishonor to France that really could be done without!"

So we brought dishonor to our country by trying to preserve for it a few valid positions in Southeast Asia, whose future now appeared to be a crucial one in the evolution of the world.

As to our cultural establishments, maintaining them seemed at first likely to give satisfaction to all. In spite of difficulties and chicaneries, some of them continued their activities for several years. These were the Saint-Paul clinic; the Franco-Vietnamese hospital, directed by a French professor (who was also in charge of the Hanoi medical school); the Franco-Vietnamese Cancer Institute, directed by French specialists; the celebrated Far East college called *L'Ecole française d'Extrême-Orient;* and the Lycée Albert-Sarraut, which, in the spring of 1956, still had eighteen hundred Vietnamese pupils and twenty or so French professors and about the same number of Vietnamese professors. At this lycée the teaching of the French language figured significantly in the curriculum.

Attached to the French lay mission, the Lycée Albert-Sarraut continued its work until April 28, 1965. By that time numerous restrictions had reduced the teaching of the French language and related subjects to a ridiculously low point, which justified the feelings of those who thought it was useless to maintain this French establishment. The lycée therefore closed its doors. With it disappeared the last witness to the cultural achievements of France in Vietnam—an important witness, for that school had attracted to it many brilliant and devoted teachers.

The lycée was a witness to French culture, but it was also a witness to the culture acquired by many Vietnamese. This establishment, which had been directed with such zeal by an obstinate rearguard comprised of a handful of teachers in 1965, closed its doors quietly in a climate of indifference.

Thus, by the year 1966, when France at last recognized the Democratic Republic of Vietnam and, *ipso facto,* the diplomatic reciprocity so long desired, the representation of France in its former colony was reduced to a general delegation. After my departure this delegation exercised its functions *ad interim* in conditions less and less favorable to a real Franco-Vietnamese entente.

The time will soon come when both the French and the Vietnamese will reproach themselves for this divorce and will realize its absurdity.

Without again trying the case of the colonial war, we can say that this war rendered the resumption of normal relations between France and Vietnam almost impossible. Viewed objectively, it is apparent that if our efforts to establish friendly relations failed, both countries must share the blame, but I believe the Vietnamese were more to blame than the French. After all, they were in their homeland, and if they had really wanted to retain us there, they could have done so by creating more favorable conditions. They did not do so. On the other hand, it is regrettable and surprising that France, after having waged a war to keep all or part of her possessions in Indochina, practically gave up any hope of maintaining some kind of presence there after Dienbienphu and the Geneva Conference.

The least disabused of the Frenchmen in charge of French enterprises retreated to South Vietnam and tried to pursue their activities there, but they went without illusions and only in the hope of postponing for as long as possible the moment when they would have to give up. Their hearts were no longer in their work.

This state of mind, this discouragement, led to a veritable complex of renunciation, which quite naturally led France to abdicate in South Vietnam as well, abandoning all the responsibilities that we still held.

This double retreat of France could not fail to create a vacuum in Indochina. On both sides of the precarious line of partition created at Geneva to arrange a cease-fire this vacuum was filled: to the North by a régime that embraced a hard-line Marxist orthodoxy; to the South by the United States, champions of anticommunism. The Ely-Collins

agreement of December 13, 1956, sanctioned this transfer.*
The future adversaries were in their places. . . .

The Hanoi government did not wait for the Ely-Collins
pact to reproach us for our disengagement, first in the North
(their reproaches here were not devoid of irony) and also in
the South (their dossier there was a bit more solid).

Let us consider the nonexecution of the agreements
reached at the Geneva Conference in July, 1954. The essential clause from the viewpoint of North Vietnam was, of
course, the one stipulating that on July 20, 1955, one year
after the signing of the accords, there should be a preelec-
toral period of twelve months opened by a conference that
would bring together the representatives of the North and
the South. One year later, in July, 1956, the Vietnamese population would be consulted on the subject of reunification.
Neither elections nor conference took place. With the excuse
that his government had not signed the Geneva Accords,
Ngo Dinh Diem obstinately opposed the idea of free elections and was supported in his feelings by the United States.

The apprehensions of the South Vietnamese government
can be understood. No doubt the idea of confronting such
a test was terrifying, for that government's adversaries in the
North were past masters in obtaining a 99 percent majority
in "free elections." The United States had also not signed the
Geneva Agreements and were perhaps right in buttressing
South Vietnam against communism. But the attitude of the
United States had other consequences, which would be recognized as serious before too long.

---

* General Paul Ely, the French Chief of Staff in Saigon, in March,
1954, informed President Eisenhower that only a massive American
intervention could save France from defeat at Dienbienphu. General
J. Lawton Collins was President Eisenhower's Special Ambassador to
Saigon.—*Translator's note*

The conflict that still, at this writing, exists not only between North Vietnam and the United States but also among the North and South Vietnamese themselves is the most serious of those consequences. But the reunification that was the goal in July, 1954, is still the supreme goal not only of Hanoi but of the great majority of the Vietnamese people, no matter what their origin or political opinion.

In a long report I made on December 26, 1954, I specified my viewpoint on this subject and sounded the alarm:

> It is indeed undeniable that any policy tending to confirm the partition of Vietnam *by opposing free elections carries within it the seeds of a new conflict.* I have said and I repeat that the Democratic Republic of Vietnam broke with us at Fontainebleau and fought us for eight years to affirm the absolute need for a unified Vietnam. Now that she is victorious she will not abandon that objective. If threatened and encircled, as it now appears she will be, she will perhaps modify her methods but not her goals.

Fifteen years later, in Ho Chi Minh's last will and testament and in the funeral oration pronounced by Le Duan, first secretary of the party, that reunification was the point stressed and acclaimed by all present.

The failure to respect the agreements of the Geneva Conference brought other consequences. One was the deterioration of relations between France and Hanoi, whose government held us responsible for Ngo Dinh Diem's refusal and reproached us for not having forced him to observe the engagements to which we subscribed. This, joined to the bitterness of North Vietnam over our refusal to accord Hanoi diplomatic reciprocity, led to the rapid deterioration of the entente that existed in 1954, which I can verify by the effects it had on my personal relations with Ho Chi Minh.

At the beginning of my mission it had been extremely easy to have conversations with the President of the Democratic Republic of Vietnam, who always made himself accessible whenever I expressed the desire to see him. Gradually it became more and more difficult to speak to him. More often I had to work out the problems that arose between us with Pham Van Dong or some other minister. The good will shown at the beginning of our extended negotiations was followed by delays and postponements that complicated everything and settled nothing. Every interview and every conference ended with an allusion to the Geneva Accords that had not been respected or the diplomatic reciprocity that was constantly deferred, and these references were made in a tone that could only worsen our relations. From the *de facto* doyen of the diplomatic corps I sank to the level of consul in Indochina.

Yet we never went so far as to break off relations between France and Vietnam. Ho Chi Minh's desire to maintain friendly relations with France was real, and it somehow surmounted other tests. In 1956 the Hungarian affair, which bore within it all the necessary justifications for a rupture of diplomatic relations, was perhaps the most significant if not the most serious of these tests.

In Hanoi at that time (as in other cities of North Vietnam) there were, besides Russians and Chinese, a number of technicians from the Communist countries of eastern Europe, sent by their respective governments to aid the "friendly" Vietnamese in running factories, hospitals, and so forth and to teach courses in technology in the schools and colleges.

At the time of the insurrectional movements in Poland against Soviet domination, in 1956, certain Poles in Hanoi had let it be known, by cautious approval of their compatriots' rebellion, that they were not as good Communists as one might suppose. I recall one day when we were visiting the Bay of Along in a junk (an excursion I had long wanted to take, which was allowed us only under the surveillance of a "guide");* we were surprised, upon entering a cave, to see the word *Poznan** traced there in large letters that had been brushed on the wall with red paint, still fresh. (Possibly the word had been put there by a group of three young, blond fellows, obviously East European technicians, whom we had passed as we entered the cave; their faces were wreathed in smiles.)

The excitement caused by that word painted on the cave wall is hard to convey. We were over six thousand miles from Poland, and no news other than official news reached Tonkin without being subjected to strict censorship. Besides, in Hanoi we were so victimized by propaganda that if we had had no personal source of information we would sometimes have doubted that there were any countries in the world other than Communist countries or those that aspired to be. Amusingly enough, our Vietnamese guide, who knew nothing about Poznan and what the mining town in Poland symbolized for us, gazed with total indifference at the seditious inscription. Had he known its meaning, it would have made him jump.

Shortly after this, in the autumn of 1956, there occurred the uprising in Budapest and its brutal and bloody suppression—prefiguring the events in Czechoslovakia sixteen years later. The uprising had effects on the Hungarians in Hanoi

---

* The "guide" soon noted that I knew those waters better than he did, for I had often navigated them in earlier years.

** Poznan is a highly industrialized city of Poland, in which the first anti-Soviet movements occurred.

that were more emphatic even than those manifested by the Poles; some of the Hugarians boldly celebrated in Hanoi the liberation movement in their country.

After the crushing of that movement by Soviet tanks and the repressive measures that followed, the Hungarians in Hanoi who had compromised themselves too openly were recalled to Budapest in terms that left no doubt as to the kind of reception they would receive. Eight of these Hungarians—three men, two women, and their three children—decided not to comply with the order and came to me to request asylum.

In the better-informed circles of the North Vietnamese capital the affair acquired considerable importance when, refusing to yield to all threats, I kept the eight fugitives under the protection of France by giving them asylum. The validity of the asylum was admittedly questionable because of the imprecision at that time of the diplomatic relations between Paris and Hanoi.

Closely confined within the limits assigned to the General Delegation of France—a kind of campus on which were situated several villas—our protégés became more and more impatient and anxious while I searched in vain for ways to save them. At first I tried all the legal and conciliatory expedients. Notably, I wrote to Ho Chi Minh (since I could no longer see him), appealing to his understanding. There was no reply. As for Minister of Foreign Affairs Ung Van Khiem, he kept repeating that the Hungarians should first obey their government and put themselves in the hands of their consul. (Our own minister of foreign affairs, to whom I sent urgent cables, did not reply at first, and when he did reply it was with pious, evasive words.)

Our ambassador in India, Stanislas Ostorog, tried hard to help me in this matter, asking the Indian government to give asylum to the Hungarians or, more exactly, to ask the Democratic Republic of Vietnam to turn them over to India as technicians. He received only empty promises.

The Canadian representative of the International Control Commission in Hanoi assured me that his country would welcome the Hungarians, but he did not provide means for transporting them. There was not a single train or plane leaving Hanoi except toward a Communist country, their destination being Peking or Moscow. The I.C.C. and the French Delegation each disposed of only one plane, which assured their supplies and liaison with the free world (South Vietnam, Laos, Cambodia), but the Hungarians could not be embarked on these without meticulous control.

I thought I had solved the problem when the Hungarians agreed to my suggestion to be naturalized. Hanoi, I felt, would hardly dare to attack French citizens. But when I saw Ung Van Khien once more and announced this news to him, this usually affable man lost his perpetual smile.

"French citizens or not," he fumed, "your protégés will not ever be allowed to leave the General Delegation of France!"

Rarely does one see an Asian lose his self-control. Ung Van Khien's anger proved that I had to take the threat seriously, and it convinced me of the necessity of saving the Hungarians by more direct means.

Among other stratagems I considered taking the chance offered us by a French cargo boat that had put in at the Haiphong harbor en route to China. The captain, with whom I managed to have a secret conversation, agreed to take his ship off course a few weeks later upon his return from China and to wait for and embark our refugees at a point agreed upon in the Gulf of Tonkin. Even if we managed to take the Hungarians to Haiphong, there was no question of embarking them in full view of everyone. We thus had to find a Chinese junk to transport them out to sea to the rendezvous point, which would involve the complicity of a Vietnamese or Chinese fisherman. None of the fishermen with whom we discussed this—very cautiously—would agree to take the risk.

After considering other plans and dropping them as impracticable, I decided, with the help of my colleagues, to hide the Hungarians in empty gasoline drums and to load them on our plane, which was flying empty to Laos. *

The children caused some difficulties, for in spite of the sedatives one of our doctors gave them, they were not completely asleep and let out some whimpers from the bottom of their uncomfortable hiding places. To cover that sound the chauffeur of our truck made his engine roar whenever he had to stop at a checkpoint on the road to the airport to show his pass and allow his cargo to be inspected according to the rules.

In short, thanks to the truck driver's coolheadedness and to our plane crew, who managed to distract the attention of the Vietnamese sentinels, the Hungarians, still in their gasoline drums, were embarked on the plane and, when airborne, were able to stretch their legs in the cockpit. Thus they were spared the imprisonment or worse that ominously awaited them in Hanoi or Budapest.

The irritation of the Vietnamese was boundless when they were unable to discover—and they did not find out for a long time—how the Hungarians had managed to slip through their fingers. * *

---

* This was our plane's last flight. The craft was taken afterward by Saigon for administrative reasons, and it was being deprived of a plane that restricted our freedom of movement still more and made me decide to cut short the negotiations.

* * This story became public property only in 1967 when quoted in

Although our relations with the Hanoi government and my personal relations with Ho Chi Minh had by that time reached their lowest point, a kind of countersign of silence surrounded this affair, and a breakdown of the negotiations was avoided. No doubt Ho believed that good relations with France were more useful to him than the carrying out of sanctions against the Hungarian citizens, who had made the mistake of thinking that a more liberal régime was about to be established in their native land. Later on I took occasion to tell Ho that I felt he would have acted as I did, had he been placed in a similar situation. He chose not to answer me.

Jean Lacouture's *Ho Chi Minh*. Lacouture had the story from me. It should be added that the eight Hungarians have settled happily in France.

joined us. When Ho Chi Minh left in his turn, we continued the conversation.

General de Gaulle had written a letter for me to deliver to Ho Chi Minh, and when I handed it to him he read it quickly and burst out laughing. His laughter was caused by a passage in which General de Gaulle specified, in diplomatic terms, that the letter would introduce me to the President of the Democratic Republic of Vietnam.

"Introduce you to me!" Ho exclaimed. "That's really unnecessary. I believe we know each other pretty well—and have known each other for some time!"

A little later, in the same jesting tone, he remarked on my habitual way of addressing him.

"Come, come!" he said. "Stop calling me *Monsieur le Président!* Between us that's ridiculous!"

As a matter of fact, General de Gaulle's letter greatly pleased Ho Chi Minh. It eased the disappointment he had felt in 1946, when he had been unable to meet the leader of the free French in Paris, and his satisfaction showed between the lines of his letter in reply, which he entrusted to me to hand to the President of the French Republic.

It was during our *tête à tête* that we broached the major issue: the war that was tearing all Vietnam apart. In terms he tried to moderate the old fighter explained the reason for his confidence in a final victory. His confidence clearly rested on his certainty that the United States, like all "invaders" of Vietnam in the past who had tried to subject the country, would become weary of the conflict. Besides, Ho was convinced that the Vietnamese people would be able to endure the burden of this war for as long as need be.

I told him that no doubt he was right if his adversaries did no more than maintain their actual pressure, but perhaps things would turn out otherwise if they threw a larger part of their armed forces into the fight.

When he answered, in a grave voice, I was reminded of his calm resolve twenty years earlier as he envisioned the perspective of a Franco-Vietnamese war.

"We know the power of our enemies," he said in that steady voice of his, as I listened in anguished silence. "We know that the Americans, if they like, can wipe out this city, as they can wipe out all the principal towns of Tonkin: Haiphong, Nam-dinh, Bao-ninh, all the others. We expect it, and, besides, we are prepared for it. But that does not weaken our determination to fight to the very end. You know," he added after a brief pause, "we've already had the experience, and you have seen how that conflict ended."

In this allusion to his victory over the French, there was no hint of sarcasm or vanity but merely the reminder of a precedent that bolstered his confidence.

He continued in this vein, predicting with cool resolution and tranquil assurance the spread of the war, the reinforcement of the American war potential, and the complete destruction of the great cities of North Vietnam that could ensue. He did not allude to the eventual destruction of the Red River embankment, but this possibility must have haunted his mind. The long pauses that marked the course of this conversation, as well as the words themselves, left unsaid many thoughts that were clearly implied.

I realized then that I had, facing me, a man of courage, who remained a lucid thinker but who was perhaps bewildered by the frightening conflict in which he was engaged. The flash of anxiety in his eyes when we shook hands and parted at the end of this interview remained in my memory for many days, bringing with it the feeling that perhaps the old fighter might sometimes wonder if he had struggled all these years merely to see his country become a mass of ruins.

Three years later, on September 9, 1969, a few hours after the funeral services for Ho Chi Minh and in the same room of the palace in which I had had my last meeting with the great Vietnamese leader, I had a long talk with Pham Van Dong.

Although sorely tried by the absence of the man in whose shadow he had so long existed, Pham Van Dong had asked for this meeting. He talked with me about the two major preoccupations that remained for him and his country: the war and the reunification of the country. He spoke with the same resolution, the same intransigence, and almost in the same terms used by Ho Chi Minh during our interview of 1966, which I have just recounted. This similarity confirmed what I had already suspected: it is vain to expect a change of policy because of a change in leadership.

The succession was assured.

Perhaps I can now relate two anecdotes, one about Ho Chi Minh and the other about Pham Van Dong. No matter how brilliant are the destiny and actions of a famous man, it is always the more inaccessible humanity in him that intrigues us even more than his public figure.

The private life of men like Ho Chi Minh or Pham Van Dong (it is impossible to speak of the one without speaking of the other) does not count, and it is not by trying to uncover it that we will find out their way of feeling. But I chanced to learn two things about them, trifling but all the same of significance. These trifles shed light on their "humanity" and particularly on their feelings toward France, that country they had so hated in its role as a colonial power but whose culture they admired, the France that had contributed a little and sometimes a great deal to their ability to fight the French.

Ho Chi Minh, who only recently was denounced by a certain newspaper as "the greatest enemy of France," asked me, a short time before his death, to procure for him a collection of phonograph records of Maurice Chevalier. He wanted especially his songs that were currently most popular in Paris. The story seems to be too good to be true, but it is true.

Unlike his master, the Premier (at this writing) of the Democratic Republic of Vietnam, Pham Van Dong, did not know France until 1946, when he arrived there as head of the Vietnamese parliamentary mission, the "good will" mission that preceded the conference at Fontainebleau. We often lunched and dined together, and one day I took him to the Tour d'Argent restaurant for a private dinner. Our table was near the window, and we had a perfect view of Nôtre Dame Cathedral, the Seine, and the Ile de la Cité. The month was April, and the weather was fine. In short, it was a day of grace, and the spectacle before us was famous and admirable.

After a moment Pham Van Dong stopped talking and sank into a contemplative silence. When he turned back from the window to me, his eyes were clouded with emotion.

"Do you know," he said, "I have just realized why those compatriots of mine who came here in the past could never forget this country."

At Fontainebleau a few weeks later, Pham Van Dong was nevertheless the most intractable of all the speakers, and he was the one who finally took the initiative of breaking off the negotiations. It was a rupture heavy with consequences.

APPENDIX 1

LAST WILL AND TESTAMENT OF PRESIDENT HO CHI MINH

DEMOCRATIC REPUBLIC OF VIETNAM
Independence—Liberty—Happiness

In the patriotic struggle against American aggression, we shall certainly have to endure the greatest tribulations and will have to consent to new sacrifices, but total victory is inevitable.

It is absolutely certain.

When that victory comes, I propose to make a tour of the North and South to congratulate our compatriots, our cadres, and our heroic combatants, and to pay a visit to our old, our young, our beloved children.

Then, in the name of our people I will visit the Socialist countries, the fraternal countries throughout the world, to thank them for having aided and wholeheartedly supported our people in their patriotic struggle against American aggression.

Tu Fu, the well known poet of the T'ang epoch, has written: "In all time, rare have been those who attained the age of seventy."

167

This year, having celebrated my sixty-ninth birthday, I have become one of those "rare" people. My mind is still lucid, but my health has somewhat failed in comparison with the preceding years. As one lives beyond sixty-nine summers, the more one ages and the more good health withdraws. This is not at all surprising.

But who can predict for how much longer I will be able to serve the revolution, the country, and the people?

For this reason I am writing these few lines in expectation of the day when I shall go to rejoin the venerable Karl Marx, Lenin, and our revolutionary elders; thus our compatriots throughout the country, the comrades of the party, and our friends throughout the world will not be caught by surprise.

To begin with, I shall speak of the party. Thanks to the close union it has realized and maintained within itself, thanks to its complete devotion to the working class, the people, and the fatherland, our party has always organized and directed our people, inducing them to fight with ardor and leading them from one victory to another.

Unity is an extremely precious tradition of our party and our people. Let all our comrades, from the members of the Central Committee to our comrades of the basic cells, cherish the unity of the party.

Within the party the best way to consolidate and develop unity is to practice a liberal democracy by regularly and seriously encouraging criticism and self-criticism. For this there must be a real bond of affection uniting all the comrades.

We are a party in power. Each member, each cadre, should thoroughly imbue himself in *revolutionary morality*, must earnestly show proof of application, thrift, integrity, uprightness, a total dedication to the public cause, and exemplary unselfishness. The party must be preserved in all its purity so as to be worthy of the role it plays as the faithful guide and servant of the people.

The members of the "Worker Youths" groups and our young people are generally of excellent character, eager to carry out *avant-*

garde tasks, not at all afraid of difficulties, and tirelessly aiming at progress. Our party should instill in them an elevated *revolutionary morality*, training them to be the continuers of socialism and to be both "Reds" and "experts."

Our working people in the plains as in the mountainous regions have endured countless privations and hardships for many centuries; they have been exploited and feudalized and have suffered colonial oppression, in addition to suffering many years of war.

Nonetheless, our people have shown great heroism and courage, ardent enthusiasm and a great application in their work. The people have always followed the party and have remained faithful to it.

The party should establish a good *plan* for economic and cultural development, in view of *constantly raising* the living standards of the people.

The war of resistance against American aggression may be prolonged. Our compatriots may have to consent to new sacrifices in property and human lives. No matter what, we must be resolved to combat the American aggressor until total victory is ours. *Our rivers and mountains and men will be here forever. The Yankees having been defeated, we will build up our country much finer than ever.*

No matter what the hardships and privations, in the end our people will surely conquer. The American imperialists will surely take to their heels. Our fatherland will surely be reunited. Our compatriots of the North and of the South will be reunited under the same roof. Our country will then have the distinction and honor of being a small nation that, through heroic combat, vanquished two great imperialisms—the French and the American—and brought a worthy contribution to the national liberation movement.

In regard to world-wide communism. Having dedicated my life to the service of the revolution, I am all the more proud to see the international Communist and workers' movement expand, and I suffer all the more because of the dissension that at present divides the Communist powers.

I want our party to do its best to contribute efficaciously to the reestablishment of good relations between the Communist powers, on a Marxist-Leninist and international proletarian basis, always in conformity with the demands of the mind and heart.

I firmly believe that the fraternal parties and countries will one day be reunited.

As to personal affairs. Throughout my life I have served the fatherland, the revolution, and the people with all my heart and strength. Now that I am about to leave this world, I have nothing with which to reproach myself. I merely regret that I am unable to serve longer and better.

I hope there will be no great funeral ceremony after my death. I do not want to waste the time and money of the people.

Lastly, I bequeath my unlimited affection to all our people, to our party, to our armed forces, and to my young nephews and nieces.

Likewise, I address fraternal greetings to my comrades, friends, and the youth and children of the world.

My ultimate desire is that all our party and all our people, closely united in combat, will raise up a Vietnam that is peaceful, unified, independent, democratic, and prosperous. Thus we will make a worthy contribution to world revolution.

(signed) Ho Chi Minh
Hanoi, May 10, 1969.

APPENDIX 2

FUNERAL ORATION

Read by Comrade Le Duan,
First Secretary of the Central Committee
of the Workers' Party of Vietnam,
at the Memorial Service for
President Ho Chi Minh

Compatriots, combatants throughout the nation, comrades, friends,

Our beloved and venerated Ho Chi Minh is no more!

We have suffered an immense loss. Our grief is boundless.

Our people and our party have lost an inspired leader and a great teacher.

The international Communist movement, the movement of national liberation, and all progressive humanity have lost an experienced fighter, a comrade resolute in battle, beloved of all.

Throughout the nation our compatriots and combatants are thinking of him, their hearts wrung with unspeakable grief. Our brothers and friends throughout the world share our grief and our poignant sadness.

171

For sixty years, ever since his early youth and until his last moment, President Ho Chi Minh dedicated his whole life to the revolutionary work of our people and the peoples of the world. His life was full of trials and sacrifices; it was one of the noblest, richest, and purest of lives.

Inspired by ardent patriotism, President Ho Chi Minh came early to Marxism-Leninism, which provided him with a beacon to light the way to the national welfare and happiness of the people. He was the first Vietnamese to apply Marxist-Leninist principles, adapting them creatively to conditions in our country; he was the first to trace the route to be followed by the Vietnamese revolution, enabling it to move forward with assured steps, leading it from victory to victory.

President Ho Chi Minh was the founder, leader, and educator of our party, the founder of the Democratic Republic of Vietnam and of the unified National Front, the beloved father-founder of the People's Army of Vietnam. He was the soul, the standard-bearer of our party, leading our people, our armed forces, uniting them *en bloc* in a heroic combat that is filling the most glorious pages of our history.

Our country, our people, our rivers and mountains gave birth to Ho Chi Minh, the great national hero, and he, in return, enhanced the glory of our fatherland, our people, and our rivers and mountains.

Ho Chi Minh is the symbol of the finest quality possessed by the Vietnamese people: that flawless indomitability the Vietnamese have forged in the course of the four thousand years of their history. Nothing is more precious than independence and liberty. It is better to die than to lose our fatherland and be reduced to slavery. The name Ho Chi Minh is a vibrant appeal for the national well-being of our country at this time; it is the message of our ancestors echoing down the centuries; it is the sacred duty that we have assumed toward future generations.

Ho Chi Minh said: "The Vietnamese nation is one and indivisible." And he said: "The South's flesh and blood is Vietnamese flesh and blood." During his lifetime he followed the liberating revolution of the South step by step, day and night. He thought of our compatriots and combatants of the South and cherished for them a boundless affection.

In bidding him farewell, we pledge ourselves solemnly: *without fail to wave the flag of national independence, determined to fight and conquer the American aggressors, determined to liberate the South, defend the North, reunify the country; we will do all this to realize the hopes he nourished.*

Liberty for the fatherland and happiness for the people—such were the most cherished aspirations of Ho Chi Minh.

He said: "I have but one desire, a passionate desire, and it is to act in such a way that our country will recover its entire independence, our people will enjoy their liberty, our compatriots will have enough to eat, clothes to wear, and be educated at school."

In his lifetime he kept a warm affection for our compatriots: the old, the young, the infants, the men and women in both the North and the South, those of the plains and those of the mountains. Before his death he bequeathed "to all the people, all the party, all the armed forces, all youths and children, boundless affection."

In bidding him farewell, we pledge ourselves solemnly: *to continue to fight with all our strength to accomplish the noble ideals of socialism and communism, ideals outlined by Ho Chi Minh for our worker class and our people, with a view to building the prosperity of our country and the happiness of our compatriots.*

President Ho Chi Minh was constantly preoccupied with and intent on edifying our party, to make of it a solid bloc, firm and powerful, completely unified. He said: "The strength of the party resides in its unity and its singleness of aim." In his person he represented the union of the nation, the ties of blood that unite the North and the South. He said: "To unite, to unite still more, to unite in the largest sense of the word is our goal! To conquer, always to conquer, to conquer in the most decisive way possible!" He never ceased to recommend and develop our tradition of unity and the affection that binds us to our compatriots and our comrades of the party.

In bidding him farewell we solemnly pledge ourselves: *to apply ourselves wholeheartedly to the preservation of unity of the party and to reinforce the combativity of our party, to make of it a unifying element binding all our people together so as to assure total victory of the revolution of our working class and our people.*

President Ho Chi Minh is the purest symbol of authentic patriotism linked closely with proletarian internationalism. His heart and mind were continually at the service of the Vietnamese people and at the service of the working class and the oppressed peoples of the world. Faithful disciple of Karl Marx and Lenin, he was not only a great patriot but also an experienced combatant in the international Communist movement and the national liberation movement of the twentieth century. President Ho Chi Minh constantly recommended that we preserve unity on the international plane, in the interest of the great revolutionary work of our country, and fulfill our sacred duties to world revolution.

In bidding him farewell, we solemnly pledge ourselves: *to develop constantly the pure internationalist sentiments that always inspired President Ho Chi Minh; to contribute wholeheartedly to reestablish and reinforce union within the Socialist camp and between the Communist powers, on the basis of Marxism-Leninism and proletarian internationalism; to tighten again the bonds of solidarity and friendship with the Indochinese peoples; to sustain with all our strength the revolutionary movements of other peoples; to contribute efficaciously to the world-wide struggle for peace, national independence, democracy, and socialism.*

So long and beautiful was Ho Chi Minh's life that it will always be a radiant example of revolutionary fervor and tenacity, of independence and national sovereignty, of profound love for the people, of total objectivity, of modesty and simplicity. He recommended that we "preserve the party in its total purity, faithful to its role as leader and servant of the people."

In bidding him farewell, we solemnly pledge ourselves: *to devote our whole life to following his example in working methods and revolutionary morality, to strengthen our minds and our revo-*

*lutionary qualities, not fearing either the difficulties or the sacri-
fices, to mold ourselves to become faithful combatants for the people and for the party, worthy to be the comrades and disciples of
President Ho Chi Minh. In his example, we will persuade our
people and our youth to set as their goal to become new men,
teachers of their country and of the new society that will plant
the flag of Ho Chi Minh.*

President Ho Chi Minh is no more with us in the flesh, but he
has left us a particularly precious legacy, the epoch of Ho Chi
Minh, the most radiant and glorious epoch in our history—the
era of independence, freedom, and socialism in our country.

All the Vietnamese people will forever keep in their hearts the
memory of the immense services he rendered.

To the spirit of the departed President Ho Chi Minh we solemnly pledge ourselves to remain faithful to him all our lives; to
work wholeheartedly and with all our strength to stand together,
firmly united; to fight with total abnegation, determined to fulfill our sacred duties in order to obtain independence and freedom
for our country and happiness for the people; and to contribute
worthily to the revolutionary struggles of the peoples in the world.

President Ho Chi Minh is no longer with us in the flesh, but he
will forever be our guide. His spirit is forever present at our side,
for we continue to follow the route he traced, and we will complete the great work he began. He lives eternally with the rivers
and mountains of the country, and his name is graven, from day
to day, ever more deeply in our hearts.

Beloved comrades and compatriots, before departing, *Bac Ho*
left a historical last will and testament for our party, our compatriots, and our fighters in both the North and the South. In
that testament are his last recommendations, his last expression
of the sentiments and the convictions he cherished toward us of
this generation and those of future generations.

Let us continue to seek to be worthy of him!

Let us contain our grief in order to struggle heroically, driving
boldly ahead, surmounting all obstacles and hardships, with com-

plete resolve to conquer definitely the American aggressors and to build socialism, thus fulfilling the pledge of honor that we pronounce in these solemn hours of farewell.

President Ho Chi Minh, the great leader, the beloved and venerated teacher of our party and our people, will live forever!

APPENDIX 3

CHRONOLOGY OF IMPORTANT EVENTS THAT AFFECTED THE MODERN HISTORY OF VIETNAM

From June 14, 1940, to September 3, 1969

June 14, 1940   Defeat of France in World War II. (Consequent weakening of her control of colonial possessions, especially in Indonesia.)

September 22, 1940   Japanese troops occupy Indochina. They will remain five years.

1941   Creation of the clandestine Vietminh in North Vietnam.

December 7, 1941   Japanese attack U.S. fleet at Pearl Harbor.

August 8, 1944   Liberation of Paris. General Charles de Gaulle declared Premier in new government.

March 9, 1945   Japanese attack some French tactical units, a portion of which retreat into

	China after withdrawing into the highlands of Tonkin.
March 11, 1945	Emperor Bao Dai denounces the treaty of the French protectorate and proclaims the independence of Vietnam.
May 8, 1945	End of World War II in Europe.
August 6, 1945	Americans drop atomic bomb on Hiroshima.
August 9, 1945	Americans drop atomic bomb on Nagasaki.
August 15, 1945	Japanese demand an armistice. End of World War II in Asia.
August 16, 1945	The Vietminh seize power in Vietnam and occupy Hanoi.
August 22, 1945	Jean Sainteny arrives in Hanoi to negotiate with Ho Chi Minh.
August 26, 1945	Emperor Bao Dai abdicates.
August 29, 1945	Proclamation of the independence of Vietnam. First public appearance of President Ho Chi Minh.
September 8, 1945	American troops occupy South Korea, replacing the Japanese.
March 6, 1946	Signing of Franco-Vietnamese (preliminary) accords by Ho Chi Minh and Jean Sainteny.
March 7, 1946	General Leclerc lands French troops in Haiphong.
March 18, 1946	General Leclerc enters Hanoi.

March 24, 1946	Interview between Ho Chi Minh and Admiral Thierry d'Argenlieu (Governor-General of the French protectorate), aboard the cruiser *Emile Bertin* in the Along Bay.
April 17, 1946	Preparatory conference in Dalat.
May 31, 1946	Ho Chi Minh leaves Hanoi for a conference in France.
June 12, 1946	Ho Chi Minh arrives in Paris.
July 6, 1946	Opening of the conference at Fontainebleau.
July 25, 1946	Announcement of the "federal" conference to be held in Dalat on August 1.
August 1, 1946	Suspension of the conference at Fontainebleau.
September 2, 1946	Breakdown of the Fontainebleau conference.
September 14, 1946	Proclamation of a Franco-Vietnamese *modus vivendi* conjointly signed by Marius Moutet, Minister of Colonies, and Ho Chi Minh.
September 19, 1946	Ho Chi Minh leaves France aboard the *Dumont-d'Urville*.
October 18, 1946	Ho Chi Minh talks with Admiral d'Argenlieu in Cam Ranh Bay.
October 21, 1946	Ho Chi Minh enters Hanoi.
November 20, 1946	Customs house incident in Haiphong.
November 21, 1946	Fighting stopped by the Lami-Nam accord.

November 22, 1946 The French commandment renounces Haiphong.

November 26, 1946 Jean Sainteny returns on another mission; he arrives in Saigon November 26 and in Hanoi December 2.

December 3, 1946 Interview between Sainteny and Ho Chi Minh.

December 19, 1946 The Vietminh in Hanoi attack the French. Jean Sainteny gravely wounded. Beginning of the Franco-Vietnamese war.

March, 1947 Jean Sainteny is recalled to France on the occasion of the debates in the National Assembly on the Indochinese affair. He will assist the Minister of Colonies as Delegate of the Government.

March 5, 1947 Monsieur Bollaert replaces Admiral d'-Argenlieu as Governor-General of Indochina.

December, 1947 Monsieur Bollaert begins negotiations with Emperor Bao Dai.

1948 Demarcation line set in Korea, which creates North Korea (protégé of U.S.S.R.) and South Korea (protégé of U.S.A.).

June 5, 1948 Franco-Vietnamese declaration signed at Bay of Along against the recognition of its independence; Vietnam associates itself with the French union.

April 24, 1949 Return of Emperor Bao Dai.

1950 Severe defeats of French armies at Langson and Cao-Bang.

June, 1950	North Korea invades South Korea.
June 29, 1950	Franco-Vietnamese conference at Pau.
December 7, 1950	General de Lattre de Tassigny appointed Commander-in-Chief and Governor-General in Indochina.
1951	Creation of the Lao-Dong; reconstitution of the Indochinese Communist party that was dissolved in 1945.
November 10, 1951	French victory at Hoa Binh.
January 11, 1952	Death of General de Lattre de Tassigny.
February 22, 1952	Evacuation of Hoa Binh.
April 1, 1952	Monsieur Letourneau becomes Minister of the French Community, and General Raoul Salan, Commander-in-Chief and Governor-General.
May 8, 1953	General Navarre replaces General Salan.
July 3, 1953	Maurice Dejean appointed General Delegate of France in Indochina.
May 7, 1954	Opening of the Geneva Conference.
May 7, 1954	Crushing defeat of the French army at Dienbienphu.
June 17, 1954	General Paul Ely, French Chief of Staff (based in Saigon), hopes for massive American intervention.
July 24, 1954	Signing of the accords in Geneva. (U.S.A. and Saigon do not sign.)
August, 1954	Jean Sainteny appointed General Delegate of France to Hanoi.

1956	The general elections provided for in Vietnam by the Geneva Conference are rejected by Saigon.
1956–1959	Resistance to the Saigon régime in South Vietnam. The Lao-Dong decides to aid the resistance.
1960	Creation of the F.N.L. (organized resistance) in South Vietnam.
May 17, 1961	Mai Van Bo becomes chief of the Commercial Delegation of the Democratic Republic of Vietnam in Paris.
1962	Beginning of (overt) American military intervention in Vietnam.
1963	Assassination of Premier Ngo Dinh Diem in Saigon.
August 7, 1964	President Johnson orders American bombardment of North Vietnam.
1965	First massive bombings of North Vietnam by the United States Air Force.
July, 1966	Jean Sainteny heads another mission to Hanoi.
January 27, 1967	Mai Van Bo becomes titular General Delegate of the Democratic Republic of Vietnam in Paris.
1968	Beginning of the Paris peace conference. Peace talks between Hanoi and Washington.
September 3, 1969	Death, in Hanoi, of Ho Chi Minh.

INDEX

Allessandri, General, 50, 51
Allies, 42, 45; landing at Normandy, 78
Along, Bay of, 67, 155
Americans, aided by French, 117
American-Vietnamese war, 102
Anghor, 13
Annam, 12; Chinese occupation of North, 48; French protectorate, 7, 73; North, 11, 14, 42, 53–54; proposed autonomy, 44
Annamese Mountain Chain, 6
Annamites, crew and passengers of *Latouche-Tréville*, 2
Army of Liberation of Vietnam, 46
Asia, Communist, 108; American desire to make South Vietnam a bastion of anticommunism in Southeast Asia, 114

Atomic bomb, 46
Aubrac, Raymond, 85

"Ba." *See* Ho Chi Minh.
Baclay post, 8
Ba Dinh, public square, vii; palace, ix
Bac-ninh, 86
Balcu (Crimea), 22
Bangkok, 25
Bao-Dai (Emperor, Vietnam), 39; abdication, 47; author's attempt to meet him, 50; counselor to Ho, 58–60; former emperor of Annam, x. *See also* Annam; Vietnam.
Basque Separatist movement, 75
Batignolles district, 18
Baudet, Philippe, 104
Ben Bella, 69

Berlin, 24
Bidault, Premier Georges, 70–72, 77, 107, 129
Binh-dinh, 12
Blum, Léon, 95
Borodin, Mikhail, Comintern envoy to China's revolutionary government, 22–23, 119. *See also* Russia
Bradeur d'empire, 68
Brazzaville, 44–45
British Intelligence Service, 27
British, meet Phan Van Dong, 117; support of consulate in Hanoi by embassy in Saigon, 116. *See also* Democratic Republic of Vietnam; Ho Chi Minh

Cachin, Marcel, 21; party chief, 76
Calcutta, French Mission, 47
Cambodia, 9, 44, 84
Camus, Albert, 125
Can-bo, political delegates, 117, 123–124
Canton, 22–23
Cao-bang, 32, 45
Caput, Louis, 61
Catroux, General, 31–32
Cédille, Governor, 53
Champa, absorbed by Vietnam in fifteenth century, 7, 9
Chandernagor, 49, 50
Chiang Fa-Kwei, General, 35–36, 37; Conference at Laichaw, 37
Chiang Kai-shek, 22, 23, 27–28, 34. *See also* China
China, army responsible for disarming Japanese, 48; author in charge of French military mission, 42; capitalism, 19–20; civil war, 23; common border with Vietnam, 6; Communist party, 34; oppose French reconquest of Tonkin, 9; Ho jailed by Chinese, 35; Ho's return (1938), 28–29; "Hundred Flowers," 124; Mao Tse-Tung, 32, 108; Tang dynasty, 8; traditional enemy-invader, 119–120; Vietnam under Chinese "protection." *See also* Communism; Ho Chi Minh; Sainteny, Jean; Vietnam
China, Cochin, 1, 12; conquest by French, 7, 9; declared an autonomous republic, 72–73; place in Indochinese Federation, 84; people should have decided own destiny, 101; proposed autonomy, 44. *See also* Indochina; Vietnam
Chinese document of 1882, 7. *See also* Tonkin
China Sea, 6
Chinese-Tonkin frontier, 39, 42; Japanese attempt to control, 31. *See also* Tonkin
Chou En-lai, 121
Chua, 12, 14
Chung-King, 54, 62
Chu Van Tang, 34
Clemenceau, 20
Clerget, Monsignor, 143
"Collaborationism" with Japanese, 39, 46
Collins, General J. Lawton, 152; Eisenhower's Special Ambassador to Saigon, 152
Colombey, 81
Committee of Liaison with Patriotic Vietnamese Catholics, 133
Committee of the Krestintern (Peasant International), 22
Communism, 19–24, 59; enemies

of South Vietnam, 109; Indochinese, 29; represented in Hanoi, 118; secret resistance movement, 38

Communist party, viii, x; birth, 75–76; Central Committee, 28; Chinese, 34, 36; First Congress of Indochinese Communist party (1935), 28, 55; in Asia, 32–33; in France, 56; supported Vietnamese, 83–84. *See also* France; Indochinese; Vietnam

Conféderation Générale du Travail (C.G.T.), 25

Conference, interministerial, 79–80

Confucius, 57

Congress at Tours, 21

Congress of Oriental peoples. *See* Moscow.

Couhoé, Monsignor, 134

Crépin, General, 54

Cripps, Stafford, 27

Cultural establishments, French, 150–151

Cung. *See* Ho Chi Minh.

Cuu-Quoc, National Welfare, 33

Cyrankievicz, 129

Dang Viet Chau, 136, 141, 142

Dalat, 68, 84

d'Argencé, Colonel Lefebre, 110

d'Argenlieu, Admiral Thierry, 49, 53, 72–73, 129; action often condemned, 101; in Paris, 92; proposes Dalat for conference, 68, 84; to set up meeting with Ho, 66. *See also* Ho Chi Minh; Vietnam

Das Kapital (Marx), 18, 25

Declaration of March 24, 44

Decolonialization, 56

Decoux, Admiral, 32–33; defeated by Japanese, 38

"Decree of Religious Freedom," 144–145

de Gaulle, President Charles, 44, 59, 81, 107, 116; letter to Ho, 163; return to power (1966), 113–114. *See also* Ho Chi Minh.

Democratic Republic of Vietnam. *See* Vietnam, North

De Tham, 13

Devillers, Philippe, 6

de Rhodes, Monsignor, 128

D.G.E.R., clandestine services of Free French, 41

Dienbienphu, 109, 110, 151

"Dirty war," 80

Division 308, conquered French at Dienbienphu, 110

Dong Hoi, ancient wall, 106

Dong Ming Hoi, 50

Dong Minh Hoi, 54

Ducroux, 34

Dulles, John Foster, 114

Dumaine, Jacques, 77

Duong Duc Hien, Minister of Education, 48

Elections, free, 152–153

Ely-Collins agreement of 1956, 152

Ely, General Paul, 106, 115, 118; French Chief of Staff in Saigon. *See also* Saigon.

Emancipation of all "oppressed peoples," 56

Emile-Bertin, cruiser, 67

Entente of 1954, deterioration, 155

Escoffier, 17

Famine of 1944–1945, 39

Federation, would divide Vietnam, 84. *See also* Vietnam
Ferry, Jules, 8
Fifth Congress of the International (Moscow), 25
Fontainebleau, beginning of post-Fontainebleau period, 85; breakdown of negotiations, 72, 79–80, 83; Conference, 69, 162, 166; failure of conference, 87; peaceful efforts, 86.
France, accord signed, 103; author only representative of Western nation present at Ho's funeral, viii, ix; beginning of war with Vietnam (1946), ix, x; defeat in Europe (1940), 31; Ho's early travels, 2–3; period of "French peace," 8, 10; Popular Front, 28; protectorates in Asia, 7; resistance against France, 3; Vichy France, 33; Vietnamese defeat French, 104. *See also* Ho Chi Minh; Vietnam
Franco-Chinese accords, 8, 53–54
Franco-Vietnamese accords, 54, 59, 62, 64–65, 71
Franco-Vietnamese cohabitation, five points for basis, 39
Franco-Vietnamese conflict, 102
Free French Forces, 31–32, 81–82
"A Free State in the Indochinese Federation of the French Union, 61
French Socialist party, 21. *See also* Ho Chi Minh
French Union, 84; armies retreat, 105. *See also* France; Vietnam
Funeral oration, vii, viii

Gandhi, 57
General Delegation of France, 117

Geneva Accords (Conference), 9, 83, 151–154; 1954 agreements, 104–106; partitioned Vietnam, 115–116; signed, 103
George, Lloyd, 20
Gia Long, 10
Giap, 38; belief in war, 89; cancels commemoration of 1918 armistice, 91; Minister of the Interior, 65–66; no détente, 95; welcomes author, 93
Gouin, Félix, 72, 80
Government in exile, provisional, 37
Great Britain, refuses aid to Indochina, 31

Haiphong, 9, 157; arrival of Ho, 91; Chinese unit fires on French Cruiser, 63; events in Haiphong, 94; French ordered to seize power, 92; landing of Leclerc's expeditionary forces, 62; last zone of evacuation, 105. *See also* Leclerc, General.
Hankow, 25
Hanoi, 27; accords not popular, 64, 70; arrival of first Chinese troops, 48–49; attacks on French and British, 85–87; atmosphere at beginning of Communist régime, 123; author, General Delegate of French Republic, 104, 107–110, 115–116; blessing of Americans, 60; British in Hanoi, 116–117; celebrations for Vietnamese independence, 88; Communists represented in Hanoi, 118; *de facto* recognition by North Vietnam, 109; de Gaulle grants recognition, 113; deterioration of relations with France, 153; effect of uprisings on Hungarians, 156–

157; funeral ceremonies, viii; General Morlière deputy for author in Hanoi, 91; General Wen in Hanoi, 54; Governor Cédille in Hanoi, 53; Hanoi bishop remains, 134; letter to Ho, 95–97; March 6 accords, 81–82; named capital, 47; natives leave city, 94; no diplomatic reciprocity by France, 113; palace, 129; Place du Théâtre, 46; relaxation of persecution of Catholics, 127; technicians from Communist countries of Eastern Europe, 154–155; underground galleries, 92. *See also* France; Ho Chi Minh; Vietnam

Haut-Commissariat of France, 49

Hedde, Monsignor, Bishop of Langston, 134

"He who enlightens," 35. *See also* Ho Chi Minh

Hiroshima, annihilated, 46

Histoire du Président Ho (Tran Ngoc Danh), 15

Hoa Than. *See* De Tham

Ho Chi Minh, agrees to French Union, 50–56, 84; anticipates German invasion of Russia, 33; assistant to Borodin in Canton, 22; attitude toward Roman Catholics, 130–134; books about Ho, xi–xii; ceases to be official guest of France 84–86; coexistence, 146–154; condemned to death *in absentia*, 26–27; conversion to communism, 19–20; created Intercolonial Union in Paris, 22; efforts to retain France, 137–140; eight years of war, 103; faith in cause, 164–166; family background, 11–18; founded *Le*

Paria (The Outcast), 22; Gandhi of Indochina, 57; goal to unite countries of Annam Empire, 73; Ho's simplicity, 128–130; interpreter for Americans, 38; last will and testament, 152–153; leader of Moscow faction, 118–119; letter from de Gaulle, 163; Marxist theories, 126–127; names used, 2; Nationalist as much as Communist, 101; organized Indochinese Communist party, 24–25; organized legal labor unions, 28–29; organizer of League of Oppressed Peoples in Russia, 23; poems composed in prison, 35–36; receives in Palace of Independence, 162; return to and reception in France, 73–82; return to Vietnam (1941), 32; seeks cooperation of French resistance groups, 39; signs accords with French, 63–72; Socialist activities in France, 20–21; State funeral, viii–x; taught Vietnam history in Lenin Institute, 28; union of "the three Ky," 61; visit to author's home (France), 75

Hoang Minh Giam, 52, 63, 93–95, 97

Hong Kong, 24–27, 34, 59

Hué, 12–13, 147

Hugo, 21

"Hunger March" (1930), 26

Hungarian affair, 154–159

"Hymn to the Leader," viii

India, 102

Indochina, 20, 26–27; 85; end of war, 103; clandestine network of propaganda agents set up, 23–25; regrouping of National-

Indochina (continued)
ists, 36; French collaboration with Japanese, 32–33; Chinese Federation proposed, 47; author requested to coordinate resistance against Japanese, 41–43; experience of French 1945–1954, 102; attack by Vietminh; 98; return of Ho, 90; French suppression of legal party, 29; base of operations for Japanese, 31–32. *See also* Ho Chi Minh; Vietnam

Indonesians, 6–7. *See also* Mongols

"Internationale," viii

International Commission of Control, Canada and India, 116–117

International Control Commission, (Canadian), 157

Internationalism, Soviet, 33

International, Seventh Congress of the, 28

Japan, attack on French defenses, 38; expansionism, 32; Fascist Japanese Army of occupation, 33; good will, 60–61

Khrushchev, 129

Kieu, classic of Vietnamese literature, 15

Kindu Koy, 23

Korea, 23, 106

Kosygin, at Ho's funeral, 121. *See also* Ho Chi Minh

Kuang-si province, 7, 23, 35–36, 50, 54

Kublai Khan, expansion into Vietnam stopped, 5

Kun-ming, 37, 39, 42–47, 56

Kuomingtang, 23–24, 28, 120. *See also* China

La Bataille du rail, 78

Labour party (British), 27

La Chambre, Guy, 104, 115

Lacouture, Jean, biography of Ho Chi Minh, 22, 33, 56. *See also* Ho Chi Minh

Laichau conference (1944), 37

Lami, French director of political affairs, 91

Langson affair (1884), 8

Lao Dong, vii

Laos, 42, 84; Chinese occupation of, 48; proposed autonomy, 44

Latouche-Tréville, 1–2; Ho as messboy, 3, 16

Lavritchev, Ambassador, U.S.S.R., to Hanoi, 118, 136. *See also* Hanoi; Russia

League of Oppressed Peoples, 23. *See also* Ho Chi Minh

League of the Rights of Man, 13

L'Echo du Vietnam, 19

Leclerc, General, 8–9, 62, 78, 129; changes attitude toward Ho, 81; favors Paris as meeting place, 68, 71; meets Giap; 66; sent to Indochina, 49–50, 53–54. *See also* Giap; Ho Chi Minh

Lecomte, Colonel, 62

Le Duan, first secretary of the party, vii–viii, 129

"Left-wing clergy," 133–134

Lena, Reverend Père, 142–146. *See also* Religious freedom; Roman Catholics

Lenin, 19, 125, 132

Lenin Institute, 22, 28. *See also* Ho Chi Minh

Le Paria (The Outcast), 22

"Letter to Comrade Nguyen Ai Quoc," attack on Ho, 73–74
Le Viet Huong, 144
l'Humanité (Paris), Communist daily newspaper, 19, 22, 27
Li Hsien-bien, Chinese Vice-premier, 121
Linov. *See* Ho Chi Minh
Li-Ta-Chao, 19
Lonquet, Charles, 20–21
Loseby, Frank, 27
Ly Thui. *See* Ho Chi Minh
Ly Thuy. *See* Ho Chi Minh

Mai Van Bo, chief of Commercial delegation of D.R.V., 114
Malaysia, to west of Vietnam, 6
Manuel, 41
Mao Tse-tung, 25, 32, 77, 108, 119; conversion to Communism at same time as Ho Chi Minh, 19–20
Markovitch, Professor, Mediator at Conferences of 1967, 85
Marxist doctrines, 60
Marx, Karl, 18–19, 25, 132
Marxist-Leninist thought, 120, 127
Mazé, Monsignor, Bishop of Ung Hoa, 134. *See also* Religious Freedom; Roman Catholics
Melanesians. *See* Mongols
Mendès-France, Pierre, 83, 104, 107–110, 114
Messmer, Pierre, 49
Michelet, 21
Mikoyan, Anastase, 129–130
Mission 5, 47
Mongols, expansion in Asia, 5; invasion of Vietnam, 33; Vietnamese, result of fusions of Mongols, Melanesians, and Indonesians, 6

Morlière, General, ix, 91, 95, 98
Morocco, Sultan of, 69
Moscow, 27; Congress of Oriental peoples, 22; Ho's return to Moscow, 23; fifth International Congress, 25; organization of Indochinese Communist party, 24–25. *See also* Communist party; Russia
Mountbatten, Admiral Lord, 102
Moutet, Marius, Minister of Colonies, 76, 87–89, 129

Nagasaki, annihilated, 46
Nam-dan, 12
Nam, no détente, 95–97; Minister of the Interior, 91, 94
National Committee of Liberation, 46
National Consultative Assembly of the D.R.V., 144
National Enterprise of Coal Mining in Hongay, 140–141
Nationalism, 20; Russian, 33; xenophobic, 120
Nationalist forces, X
Nationalist parties, 71; pro-Chinese, 72; two groups, 54; Vietnamese, 44–47
National Vietnam Assembly, 62
National Welfare, 33
Nehru, 129
Nghe-an region, 11–13; native province of Ho Chi Minh, 26
Ngo Dinh Diem, encouraged Catholic exodus to South Vietnam, 131; opposed free elections, 152–153; President of South Vietnam, 108
Nguyen Ai Quoc. *See* Ho Chi Minh
Nguyen Anh, 10

Nguyen Dinh Sac, father of Ho Chi Minh, 12–13
Nguyen Duy Trinh, Minister of Foreign Affairs, 161
Nguyen Hai Than, 36, 50
Nguyen Ko Thach, 162
Nguyen, lords of the South, 9–10
Nguyen Tat Thanh. *See* Ho Chi Minh
Nguyen Thanh Ha, 162
Nguyen Tong-Tam, ultra-Nationalist, 44
Nhân Dân, 144
Normandy, Allied landings, 41–42; coast, 78–79
Norodom Sihanouk, Prince, Chief of state in Cambodia, 161
Note d' Orientation, 92–93
"Notes on the revindications of Annamese people," 20
Nung province, 32

Ostorog, Stanislas, French Ambassador in India, 156
Outcast, The (*Le Paria*), 22

Palais de la Censure, 13–14
Passy, Colonel, 41, 42
Patti, Major, 47, 48
Peasant International, 22
Peking, 19; entente with Moscow, 118
Pham Ke Touai, 46
Pham Van Dong, 23, 104, 110–111; annoyed by exodus of Roman Catholics, 131; appeal to stop persecution of Roman Catholics, 134; head of Vietnamese delegation, 84; imprisoned in Poulo-Condore, 26; intervention for Père Lena, 145–146; intimate collaborator of Ho, 29; meets British, 117; mission to France, 166; premier, viii; talks with Van Dong, 161–165; tea given in author's honor, 113; urges French economic substructure remain undisturbed, 136–140. *See also* Ho Chi Minh; Jean Sainteny
Phan Anh, 136, 141
Phan Boi Chau, adversary of French colonialism, 13, 28
Phan Chau Trinh, revolutionary, 13, 21
Phan Van Truong, 21
Philippines, to the east of Vietnam, 6
Pho Trang Tri, ix
Pigneau de Béhaine, Bishop of Adran, 10
Pignon, Léon, 50–64
Poldès, Léo, 76
Populaire, 20–21
Popular Front (1936–1938), 28
Portugal, 10
Potsdam, 48, 53, 119
Poulo-Condore, 26
Propaganda, Communist, 23. *See also* Communism
Provisional government of France, 48

Red River, vii, 6
Religious freedom, 130–133, 140–144
Reunification, goal of Hanoi and people, 152–153, 165
Revolution, Nationalist, 23
Revolution, Russian, 19
Roman Catholics, in Vietnam, 127, 130–131
Russia, delegates' leadership to Chinese in Hanoi, 118; revolution, 19

Saigon, 13, 49; French and British embassies, 116; conference with General Ely, 108; message to Blum delayed, 95; office of *haut-commissaire*, 92; voyage to Le Havre, 3. *See also* Ely, General Paul

Sainte-Adresse, 16

Sainteny, Jean, appointments to North Vietnam, 107–109; 115; *Commissaire de la République* for Tonkin and North Vietnam, 50; consul in Indochina, 154; faith in Vietnamese, 102; Ho requests meeting, 43–45; in Hanoi, 47, 115–116; last meeting with Ho, 161; letter from Ho, 97–100; letter to Ho, 95–96; reciprocity granted in 1966, 114; summoned to Paris, 104; talks with Ho, 58. *See also* Ho Chi Minh

Salan, General, 71

Sarraut, Albert, 81

SEATO defense pact of Southeast Asia, 114, 115

Second International, 21

17th parallel, North, goals of French, 106

Seventh Congress of the International, 28

S.F.I.O., militant activist corps, 61

Shanghai, 25; Ho's hideout, 27; office of the Far East created, 22

Siao Wen, General, 35, 37, 54–55

Singapore, British Crown colony, 31

Simpson-Jones, Commander, 85

"Socialist realism" art, 124

Soisy-sous-Montmorency, 85

"The Student." *See* Ho Chi Minh

Sun Yat Sen, 22

Sureté (Hanoi), 27

Tang dynasty. *See* China

Teroki, Marshal, 61

Thailand, 15, 24

Thainguyen region, 38

Thanh, 33

Thanh Nien, young Communists (Vietnamese), 23

Théas, Monsignor, Ho's visit to Lourdes, 132

"Three Ky," 44, 61, 73; disagreement, 84

Thorez, Maurice, vice-president of the Council of Ministers, 71–72, 87

Third International, 21–22, 23; liaison with Moscow and French Communist party, 25. *See also* Communism

Thung-king, 9

Thuy, Citizen. *See* Bao Dai

Tientsin, 8

Tillow, Charles, Minister of Air, 80

Tong Van So. *See* Ho Chi Minh

Tonkin, vii, 6–9; attacks on "good whites," 86; author ordered to Tonkin, 92; Chinese occupation, 48–49; collapse of Chinese, 71; Colonialist atmosphere, 68; commando troops, 42; delta, 34; French protectorate, 7, 73–74; Ho's return, 89; in hands of Vietminh, 41; possible return of France, 108; proposed autonomy, 44; seizure of food by Vietminh agents, 39; subversion squelched, 35

Tonkin Gulf "incident," 102, 157

Tours. *See* Congress at Tours, 21

Tran Ngoc Danh, 15

Treaty of Versailles, 20

Trinh, lords of the North, 9–10; raised ancient wall, 106
Tsin-tsi Congress, 32–34
Tu-ve, Vietnamese "self-defense" groups, 91

"Uncle Ho," *See* Ho Chi Minh
Ung Van Khiem, 156, 157
Union des Femmes, 146
United States, did not sign Geneva agreements, 152; entered World War II, 37; hostility, 149; refused aid to Indochina, 31; would weary of conflict, 163–164
University of Oriental Peoples, 22
U.S.S.R. *See* Russia.

Vaillant-Couturier, Paul, 28
Vollup, General, 92
Versailles. *See* Treaty of Versailles.
Vichy government, 31, 44
Viet-gian, 64, 68, 90. *See also* Ho Chi Minh
Vietminh, 28, 114; agree to return of French troops, 54; attacks on Indochina, 97–98; created at Tsin-tsi Congress, 33; demands sovereignty of Vietnam be respected, 91; eliminates pro-Chinese Nationalists, 57; famine advances cause, 39; five-point message, 43; flag, 46; Ho ends stay in France, 85; Ho leader of Vietminh, 35; intensified propaganda and violence against French, 49; seize power, 86; tentative accords, 58–62; two war chiefs, 34
Vietminh League, 43, 46
Vietnam, bonds with France never broken, 102; celebrations of in-
dependence, 48, 73–75, 84, 88; demarcation line between China and India, 6; division by Geneva Accords, 9; ethnic entity in third century B.C., 6; flag, 46; free state, 64–65; geographic characteristics, 7; history of more than twenty centuries, 5; independence from colonial rule, 19–20; period of "French peace," 8; Vietnam hawks, 101; war begun, 97–100
Vietnam Cong-San Dang, or Indochinese Communist party, 25
Viet-Nam Doc Lap Dong-Minh. *See* Vietminh
Vietnamese delegation in France, 79–80, 107–108; left for Tonkin (September), 84; support of Communists, 83–84
Vietnam, North, 26, 43, 48, 108; ask French to retain their enterprises, 135–141; author General Delegate of French Republic to Democratic Republic of Vietnam, 110–112; brief period of pacification, 10; Geneva Accords signed, 103; government's proclamation on freedom of worship, 133; Nationalists, 32, 35, 37; Nature of people, 12–14; partitioned, 115–116; promise by Americans to Chinese after World War II, 9; provisional government, 58–59. *See also* Giap, Ho Chi Minh
Viet-Nam Quoc Dan Dang Association, 44, 54
Vietnam, South, division, 9; difficulties, 108–109. *See also* Bao Dai
Vinh, 26

Vinh Thuy. *See* Bao Dai
Vladivostok, 28
Vo Nguyen Giap, intimate collaborator of Ho, 29, 34. *See also* Giap
Vu Hong Khanh, Deputy Commissaire, of National Defense, 64

Wilson, 20
Workers' Party. *See* Lao Dong

World War II, France weakened, 8, 100–101; United States enters war, 37
Writing, Vietnamese, transliterated and Romanized in 17th Century, 128

Youth Corps. *See* Thanh Nien
Yunnan, 7, army, 119; province, 42, 45

Zola, 21